Parallel
Programming

Intel/McGraw-Hill Series

Published

Parallel Programming

Susann Ragsdale

Editor

McGraw-Hill, Inc.

New York   St. Louis   Auckland   Bogota
Caracas   Hamburg   Lisbon   London   Madrid
Mexico   Milan   Montreal   New Dehli   Paris
San Juan   São Paulo   Singapore
Sydney   Tokyo   Toronto

Library of Congress Cataloging-in-Publication Data

Parallel programming / Susann Ragsdale, editor.
    p.   cm -- (Intel/McGraw-Hill series)

  Includes index.
  ISBN 0-07-051186-1 : $29.95
  1. Parallel programming (Computer science) I. Ragsdale, Susann.
II. Series.
QA76.642P39 1991
004 ,35--dc20

  2 3 4 5 6 7 8 9 0   DOC/DOC   9 7 6 5 4 3 2 1

ISBN   0-07-051186-1

*The sponsoring editor for this book was Neil Levine, the
editing supervisor was Kimberly A. Goff, and the production
supervisor was Donald F. Schmidt.*

This book was set in Century Schoolbook.

Printed and bound by R.R. Donnelley & Sons.

To Rian and Bob, for all the time away from home.

Contents

Contributors

Raymond Asbury, Technical Marketing Manager, *Intel Supercomputer Systems Division* (CHAP. 4)

William L. Bain, Jr., Ph.D., Senior Staff Software Engineer, *Intel Supercomputer Systems Division* (CHAP. 7)

Michael Barton, Ph.D., Senior Computational Scientist, *Intel Supercomputer Systems Division* (CHAP. 5)

J. E. Brandenburg, Ph.D., Principal Computational Scientist, *Intel Supercomputer Systems Division* (CHAP. 6)

J. Victor Jackson, Ph.D., Field Applications Engineer, *Intel Supercomputer Systems Division* (CHAP. 1, 2)

Edward J. Kushner, Ph.D., Senior Applications Engineer, *Intel Supercomputer Systems Division* (CHAP. 3)

David S. Scott, Ph.D., Principal Computational Scientist, *Intel Supercomputer Systems Division* (CHAP. 1, 2, 5)

Preface

This book is an introduction to developing applications for distributed-memory parallel computers. The model used in the book is based on the Intel iPSC®/2 and iPSC/860 Supercomputers (referred to as iPSC systems), but the models and principles should be valid for other systems of this type.

Because interest in parallel computing arises from all quarters, it is expected that those reading this book will come from a variety of backgrounds, and the focus of their interests will also vary. There is no attempt to provide detailed programming information (although Appendix A offers code examples of some of the problems described in the book), but rather to provide clearly defined terms and a strong sense of the process and methods of parallel programming for this kind of machine.

The first three chapters are intended primarily for those who are unfamiliar with the operation and architecture of loosely-coupled parallel systems. These chapters attempt to define terms commonly applied to these systems, and to introduce the programming model and the process of programming this kind of system.

The next four chapters are intended for those who are specifically interested in developing parallel software. They focus on decomposition methods (the methods of designing software to run on a multi-processor, distributed-memory system), and provide several examples for each method that show how parallel algorithms can be derived from serial algorithms. These examples are intended to give the software developer patterns that will help determine the best decomposition method for future applications.

Chapter 1 is a brief description of the architecture of the loosely-coupled system with definitions of important concepts.

Chapter 2 describes the programming model.

Chapter 3 describes the programming process and the principles involved, using a very simple example to illustrate the process.

Chapter 4 introduces and defines the decomposition methods.

Chapter 5 provides detailed algorithmic examples and techniques of domain decomposition.

Chapter 6 offers more information on control decomposition, with algorithmic examples.

Chapter 7 introduces object-oriented programming for parallel systems.

Chapter 8 is a brief overview of some of the emerging tools for parallel software development.

Appendix A contains some of the code developed for the iPSC/2 for some of the examples shown in Chapters 5 and 6.

A Glossary summarizes the definitions of many of the terms defined in the book.

A Bibiography lists many of the relevant technical papers published by the technical staff of Intel Supercomputer Systems Division.

Acknowledgments

This book was a group effort, and could not have been done without the help of some people who already had no spare time to give. David Scott, Bill Bain, Michael Barton, Joe Brandenburg, Ed Kushner, Ray Asbury, and Victor Jackson all managed to give a lot of time in addition to their extraordinary technical expertise. Many other people, inside and outside Intel Supercomputer Systems Division also contributed their time to providing thoughtful reviews along the way. Justin Rattner deserves special mention both for technical reviews and for helping make sure the project got done.

Without the help of others, the practical aspects of creating a book from words on paper could not have been surmounted: Berit Osmundsen-Wicke who created the Intel publishing program and was the channel through which it all happened, all of the helpful people at McGraw-Hill, and Erin Sunahara, graphics artist, electronic publishing expert, and moral support throughout.

Parallel
Programming

1

The Parallel System: Divide and Conquer

Conventional computers aren't fast enough to do what you need to do. Supercomputers may not even be fast enough, and the price puts them out of range in any case. Everyone is talking about parallel computers — a bewildering array of them — and you need to know whether they will give you the performance you need at a price you can afford, and what it will take to program them

There is little question that parallel computing is the most important new technology for solving computationally intensive problems. As Dr. Kenneth W. Neves of Boeing Computer Services noted, "The ability to bring a product to market while maintaining a competitive edge requires ever-increasing computational power. For multi-year research problems involving extremely large calculations, parallel supercomputers win on performance, scalability, and even price. Large scale parallelism is the only way we are going to get the kind of performance that will let us solve the really complex problems of the next decade."

Parallel computers are also likely to be around for a long time as applications for them become more widespread. The Hamrick professor of Engineering and Director of Applied and Computational Mathematics at Princeton University, Steve Orszag, said, "Research organizations have been using parallel supercomputers like the Intel iPSC/860 for some time now, and it's just a matter of time before they proliferate throughout the industrial computing sector. Advanced computing technology... gives us the ability to ask questions and examine answers more quickly, in greater detail, and more cost effectively than ever before possible."

This book is a roadmap to parallel computing. It focuses on what you need to know to design parallel applications or port existing applications, and how to view your applications so you can produce cost-effective parallel programs. This book focuses on loosely-coupled parallel computers such as the Intel iPSC/2 and iPSC/860 Supercomputers. The principles and general models described should, however, apply to other parallel systems.

The most important difference between programming serial computers and programming parallel computers of this type lies in how you think about the problem, not in the mechanics of programming itself. Design and implementation techniques for parallel systems (called parallel *decomposition* techniques) have already been developed. You may need to change your focus, but you don't have to invent the view.

This chapter introduces you to parallel computers and the way the design of the system affects the way you program it.

Figure 1.1 Using a parallel application.

A Bird's Eye View of Parallel Systems

All parallel computers use multiple processors. The differences among types of parallel computers lie in other areas. Parallel computers are classified by two qualifiers: the relationship of the memory to the processors and the number of instruction streams available to the system.

There are two general relationships between memory and processors: *distributed memory* and *shared memory*. In distributed-memory systems, each processor has its own private memory. Shared-memory systems have a single pool of memory to which all processors have access.

The other terms that describe distinguishing characteristics of parallel computers are *MIMD* (Multiple Instruction, Multiple Data) and *SIMD* (Single Instruction, Multiple Data). (These acronyms are commonly pronounced mim-dee and sim-dee.) MIMD systems allow processors to work on separate instruction streams, or tasks, at the same time, while the processors in SIMD systems all operate on a single instruction stream simultaneously. Synchronous behavior is automatic in SIMD machines; MIMD systems require that synchronization be programmed in. A MIMD machine can simulate a SIMD machine, but not vice-versa. MIMD machines can make use of either shared or distributed memory, but only distributed memory is used in SIMD machines (multiple processors could not be used efficiently with a single instruction stream and a single memory pool).

The focus of this book is on distributed-memory MIMD systems. Systems of this kind are made up of a set of *nodes*, each of which consists of a main processor, memory, and interface to the network. Each node has the computing power of a stand-alone workstation. Nodes process information independent of one another and communicate by sending and receiving messages. This independence gives these systems what is called a *loosely-coupled* architecture.

In many respects, a distributed-memory parallel computer operates like a large corporation with divisions distributed around the world. Each division has its own goals, but all must work in close communication to operate a successful company. The corporate offices are analogous to the nodes in the parallel computer, and the fax network connecting the offices corresponds to the communications network that connects the nodes.

A loosely-coupled parallel system provides three major advantages:

• It is flexible. Nodes with different types of processors can be used to adapt the system to specialized problems.

- It is cost-effective. Parallel processing can significantly reduce the processing time for large computation-intensive problems. While some systems use specially designed components, others further reduce costs by using existing technology wherever possible.
- It is easily scalable. Loosely-coupled systems are easy to expand, and you can also run several smaller problems concurrently.

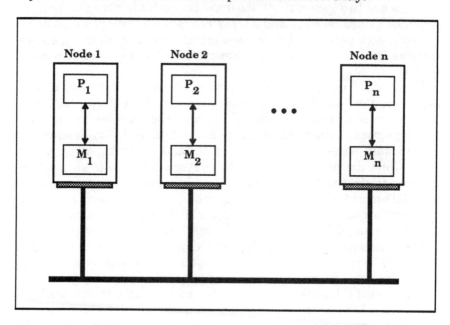

Figure 1.2 Nodes with communications network.

A Flexible System

Distributed-memory parallel computers are designed to solve a broad range of qualitatively different problems: engineering problems that require extensive numeric computations (vector, scalar, or both), artificial intelligence (AI) problems requiring extensive use of symbols, and problems that involve combinations of these. One approach is to use specialized nodes to enhance the performance on certain types of problems.

A loosely-coupled system design facilitates this flexibility. It is possible, in fact, to have a system with specialized nodes for numeric, symbolic, or input/output processing, all integrated in one system. These nodes can be programmed either to cooperate to solve a single problem, or to work on several different problems at once.

A Cost-Effective System

Systems based on a single processor execute only one instruction at a time, and so are limited by the performance of its hardware. The fastest sequential supercomputers presently operate within an order of magnitude of their theoretical maximum speed, which is on the order of 3 GFLOPS ($3x10^9$ floating point operations per second).

Sequential systems solve many large problems too slowly to be cost-effective on sequential systems; many others cannot be solved on a sequential system at all. A move to parallel systems can provide a more cost-effective solution for some problems, and a way to solve the currently insoluble. An application running on multiple processors in a parallel computer can surpass the maximum performance for sequential computers. Although the performance of each node is constrained by sequential limits, the system as a whole is not.

Some parallel systems, such as the iPSC systems, use readily-available processors to reduce the cost of the systems without incurring the enormous development costs of designing a processor for that system only. The loosely-coupled system can also take advantage of advances in sequential processor technology for ever-greater speed of execution. As new, faster processors are developed, it is possible to upgrade the performance by designing a new node based around the faster processor, rather than redesigning the entire system.

A Scalable System

A loosely-coupled parallel system makes it easy to scale the system to the problem to be solved or to upgrade the system incrementally. It is possible, for example, to start with a smaller system and expand the system as your computing requirements grow. For example, you may use the computer first to simulate air flow over an aircraft wing, later adding nodes to the system to simulate the air flow over the entire aircraft.

If your system has more nodes than a problem requires, you can scale the system by using groups of nodes for separate applications or separate users. You can fit the system to the size of the problem at hand.

A Closer Look

MIMD (multiple instruction, multiple data) distributed-memory systems are called *loosely-coupled* because each node operates as an independent system; interaction between nodes is limited to messages passed between them. This section describes what this means to the programmer.

Multiple Instructions, Multiple Data

Each node in the parallel system can be viewed as a self-contained computer. Each has its own main processor, memory, interface to the network, and, if necessary, a numeric coprocessor. Each node executes its own program and stores its own data. Even when the same code is given to each node, the program running on any node is essentially separate from what is running on other nodes.

To the program designer, this means that it is important to determine the best way to cut (or *decompose*) the problem into pieces that can then be distributed among the nodes. It also enhances the variety of ways the computer can be used to solve problems.

- A single program can be divided into different parts, with nodes executing different parts of the program
- Several separate programs can be executed at once on different sets of nodes
- A single program can be executed simultaneously by different nodes emulating a single instruction, multiple data (SIMD) machine.

Figure 1.3 illustrates the difference between the way a MIMD and a SIMD machine operate. In the SIMD system, each instruction is broadcast to all processors, and they all execute the same instruction in "lockstep." No such restrictions exist in MIMD systems.

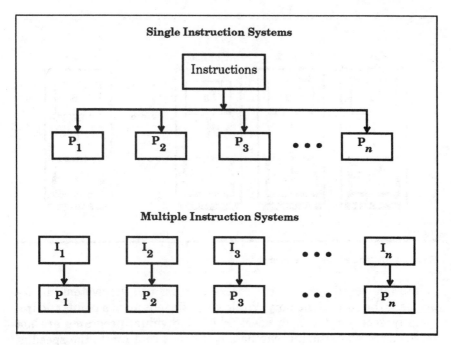

Figure 1.3 MIMD vs. SIMD operation.

Memory Schemes

The two basic memory configurations in parallel computers are *distributed* and *shared*. In a distributed-memory system, the contents of the memory on a node can only be accessed by the processor on that node (the memory is local to the node). When a process on one node requires information owned by another node, the information must be sent explicitly as a message from one node to the other. To the programmer, this means that there are no shared variables, and no way for one processor to affect another processor's data inadvertently. Figure 1.4 illustrates the distributed memory concept.

The other way to organize memory is shared memory. In a shared-memory system, the memory is global; it is in one pool that is shared by all of the processors. Parallel computers of this type generally use one of two ways to gain direct access to memory — a common system bus or a switching network.

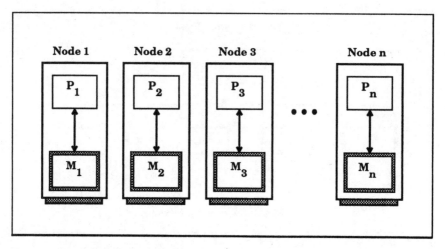

Figure 1.4 Distributed-memory systems.

In a bus-based system, all processors must use the system bus for access to the system memory. While very efficient up to a point, and frequently good for multiple users whose individual programs are not large or complex, the bus can be a bottleneck that limits the speed at which processors can access memory. This limits the number of processors that can effectively be added to the system, and therefore also limits the performance. Typical systems are limited to a few tens of processors.

The switching network was designed to avoid the memory access bottleneck by providing many different paths to memory while maintaining a single global address space. In this kind of system, the processors are connected to memory through one or more layers of switches (usually called butterfly switches), the number of layers being directly proportional to the logarithm of the number of processors in the system.

While offering greater bandwidth than a bus-based system, the switching network is susceptible to "hot spots." This is an effect that occurs when multiple memory references simultaneously compete for the same switch, causing a significant degradation of the whole network. Because the location of hot spots varies with the application program and how memory is allocated, it is difficult, in general, for the programmer to predict or avoid hot spots.

Another difficulty is that the switches through which the processors access memory introduce high and non-uniform memory access times. In fact, certain systems have redistributed memory so that each processor has a local memory bank that is also globally accessible to all other processors through the switching network. In this scheme, although all application data is globally accessible, it becomes more efficient for processors to access local data only. This greatly reduces the value of the switching network. Finally, a switching network adds complexity to the system, affecting system cost, reliability, and the number of processors that can be added to the system.

Figure 1.5 illustrates the operation of shared-memory systems.

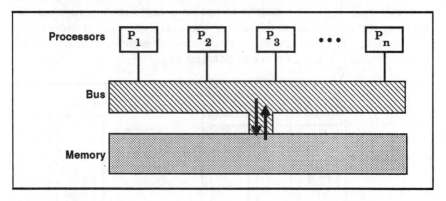

Figure 1.5 Shared-memory systems.

For many scientific applications, the distributed-memory scheme can offer higher absolute performance than shared memory, providing uniform and fast memory access times and avoiding the problem of bus contention. Distributed-memory systems are designed to be scaled to hundreds or thousands of processors without the addition of different and more complex hardware to support the expansion. The key to this is reducing or eliminating central and global resources that introduce bottlenecks or increase system complexity as the number of processors in the system increases.

All of these factors enhance the value of the loosely-coupled architecture for a wide variety of large scientific applications. To make it work, however, nodes must be able to communicate. Rather than allowing processors access to memory that is local to other processors, with a risk of corrupting data, nodes pass information to one another in the form of messages.

Communication

As explained earlier, each processor has its "private" memory, requiring the explicit transfer of data. When information that is stored on one node is required by another node, the originating node must send the information, and the node that requires it must receive it.

A message-passing network supports message traffic between nodes. Messages can convey information between nodes, and also synchronize node activities. Messages containing data or code are copies of information resident on the sending node. They are sent through the message-passing network and delivered to other nodes, as shown in Figure 1.6.

In general, the time required to pass messages is dependent on the speed of the hardware and the way the network is interconnected. A balanced system will exhibit interprocessor communication performance that is comparable to computational performance.

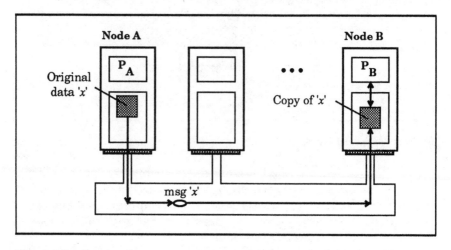

Figure 1.6 Passing messages.

Node Interconnection

In early loosely-coupled systems, the interconnection of the nodes presented some interesting problems.

It is possible to imagine many ways of building networks of processors: linear arrays, meshes, tori, hypercubes, rings, completely connected crossbars, etc. The simplest connection scheme is a simple chain, stringing all of the nodes together in a linear array, as illustrated in Figure 1.7.

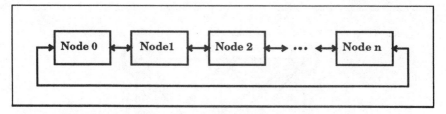

Figure 1.7 Linear array network.

A problem with the linear array (as an example) is its limited message bandwidth and the worst-case distance messages have to travel.

Other, more flexible connection schemes are available, such as the hypercube or the mesh configurations. Connection schemes like these provide a higher potential total bandwidth, and reduce the maximum distance that messages must travel. A simple hypercube is illustrated in Figure 1.8.

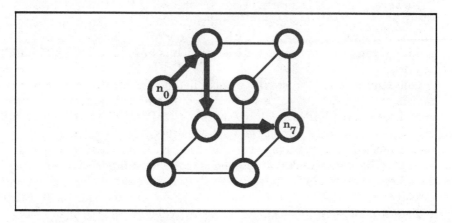

Figure 1.8 Message-passing network based on the hypercube.

Given that message traffic between nodes cannot be predicted ahead of time for all applications, the ideal network interconnection (at least from a programmer's point of view) is fully-connected, where each node is physically connected to every other node. This would guarantee that messages have a direct path to any node, which would maximize the possible number of simultaneous messages in the system (message bandwidth) and minimize the message-passing time and distance. This kind of connection is shown in Figure 1.9.

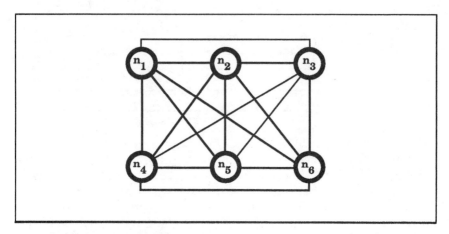

Figure 1.9 A fully-connected network.

However, such an interconnection scheme would add enormous complexity to a system, making it difficult to scale up to a large number of nodes. For example, a system with 1,000 nodes would need about half a million connections between nodes, which is impractical to build and maintain.

One approach is to make the system behave, as far as the programmer is concerned, as though it is fully-connected, while avoiding that complexity in the hardware. For example, the iPSC/860 system uses an innovation called the Direct-Connect Module (DCM) technology. It is based on the same technology used in modern telephone switching networks. When you make a telephone call, a number of electronic switches are closed in the telephone network that establish a dedicated circuit to carry the conversation. Similarly, when a message is sent to a distant node, a number of electronic switches are closed in the message-passing network to establish a dedicated circuit to carry the message.

This path does not actually go through any of the processors; instead, each node has a communication module separate from the processor that uses special switching hardware. No processor time is required from intermediate nodes. Once the circuit is established, the message travels across the network at the rate of 2.8 megabytes per second. As soon as the end of the message traverses each of the switches, the switch is free to be used for another message. Establishing the circuit requires a very small portion of the time required to pass the message due to the speed of the communications network.

Thus, although each node is *physically* connected to a limited number of other nodes directly, each node is *effectively* connected to all other nodes in the system. This makes the physical connection of the nodes of little consequence to the programmer. This is a significant change of view — from a hypercube (the hardware engineer's view) to a completely connected graph (the application programmer's view).

Summary

The technology of single-processor supercomputers has nearly reached its theoretical performance limits. To go beyond this limit to solve current and future computationally demanding applications, the next step must be a move to parallel computers. MIMD distributed-memory computers like the iPSC Supercomputers provide the kind of cost-effective performance required to solve a wide range of scientific and engineering applications.

The next chapter examines a programming model for the loosely-coupled parallel computer.

2

A Programming Model for the Loosely-Coupled Parallel System

The programming model for developing applications for a distributed-memory parallel computer has three main aspects:

- Computations are performed by a set of parallel processes.
- Data accessed by one process is private from other processes, and variables are not shared.
- Processes communicate by passing messages.

This chapter establishes this simple model and describes some of the important mechanisms involved.

Computing with Parallel Processes and Private Data

A process in a loosely-coupled parallel system is a sequential part of a complete parallel application. This sequential part runs on a single system node. To make most efficient use of a loosely-coupled parallel computer, you must design your application as a set of processes that are executed simultaneously (in parallel). The model does not restrict the number of processes or the number of processors available.

Like people working in an office, processes perform different tasks and exchange information as required to achieve the common goals of the application. These processes can be written in any appropriate supported language.

In an office, workers have their own files, and cooperate to exchange information, rather than rifling one another's desks. Similarly, the processors in a loosely-coupled parallel system operate independently of one another. As a result, processes on different nodes are executed *asynchronously* — there is no guaranteed timing relationship between them. Communication serves both to synchronize processes and to exchange code and data information among processes. The next section describes the parallel communications model.

Communicating

Communication among processes is based on a very simple model. When information from one process is required by another, the process originating the information must send a copy of the information to the receiving process in the form of a message, and the receiving process must explicitly receive it.

This is comparable in concept to a fax system, the electronic communication system used to send facsimiles of documents from one location to another. In general, sender and receiver need to know that the document is being transferred, and the sender provides the number identifying the destination, the name of the recipient, and the subject of the document. The sending fax then creates a connection to the receiving fax and sends the message, as illustrated in Figure 2.1.

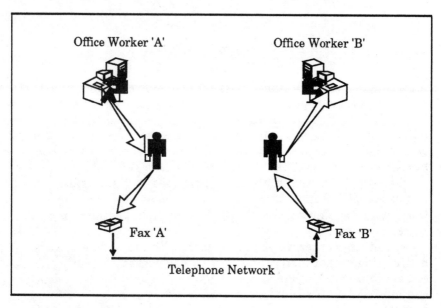

Figure 2.1 The fax systems.

Transferring messages between processes requires the same steps. To cause one process to send a message to another, you include a message-passing routine in the sending process. This routine assigns a type to the message, defines the location and length of the information to be sent, and where it is to be sent. When it is executed, a copy of the desired information (the "document") is sent to the specified node (the destination) and process (the name of the recipient). The message type (the subject) is attached to the message. The communications hardware creates the path over which the message is sent.

The process that requires the information must then receive the message that is being sent. Therefore, this process must contain a "receive" routine that identifies the type of the message it expects and where the information is to be stored until used. When the message arrives, the process can receive it.

Figure 2.2 illustrates a message sent from one process to another.

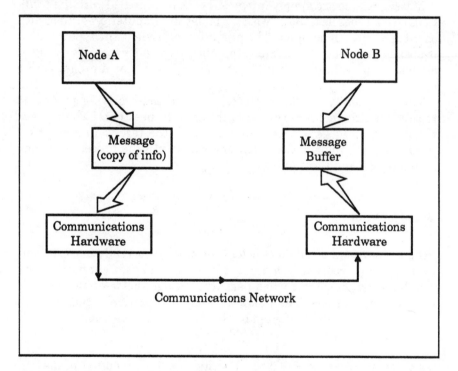

Figure 2.2 Passing messages between nodes.

It is important to remember that messages consisting of code or data are copies of the information stored in memory on the sending node. It is not a reference or pointer to the variable. Sending a pointer would be useless because of the privacy described earlier. Each process has its own code and data structures, and the receiving process does not have access to the memory on the node executing the sending process.

Message Types

For systems such as the Intel iPSC systems, the protocol for sending and receiving messages requires that each message have an identifier, or *type*. These types are integer values used to differentiate between messages. Each message is assigned a type in the send routine, and this same type must be specified in the receive routine in the receiving process. This allows the correct message to be received among all of the incoming messages.

Message types are simply integers, not to be confused with the traditional data types associated with variables in computer programs, such as integer, real, or complex. The programmer assigns the type value. It is possible to use specific values to indicate certain types of messages, allowing type values to be interpreted consistently as a programming aid.

The message type allows you to program the receiving process to receive specific messages when it is ready to use them. The cycle of receiving a message, doing some work with the received information, receiving more information, etc., continues until the process has completed its job and terminates.

Message Handling

People often send documents before the receiver is ready to read them. Perhaps more frequently, a document is required before it has arrived. Similar situations occur when passing messages between processes in parallel applications. The following sections describe details of message handling as implemented by the Intel iPSC supercomputers.

Synchronous Message Handling. Halting further execution of instructions in a process until a message is sent or received is called synchronous message handling. This is analogous to the situation where you cannot proceed with your work until you receive a needed document.

The message-passing calls include synchronous or *blocking* sends and receives. This is probably the simplest to visualize. When a process issues a request to receive a message, the process executes no further instructions (is blocked) until a message of the type expected has been received. If the message has not yet arrived at the node at the time the request is made, the process will do nothing until the message arrives. If the message had arrived at the node before the process made the request, the process would wait only until the message is copied into the process' memory from the system buffer in which it was temporarily stored.

Similarly, when a process makes a request to send a message synchronously, the process is blocked until the message is copied by the operating system from the sending process' memory into the message passing network. This does not mean that the message has arrived at its destination. It means that it is on its way, and that the memory that stored the outgoing message can now be changed if needed.

Synchronous message passing calls are essential for correct implementation of many algorithms, and are also useful for initial development and debugging of applications that will ultimately use asynchronous message passing. They also provide a convenient means of loose synchronization between processes.

Asynchronous Message Handling. Usually, while waiting for an expected document, rather than waiting around, you continue working on other projects. Then you can start working with the expected document when it arrives and you are ready for it. This corresponds to asynchronous message handling.

It is usually more efficient to handle messages asynchronously. Asynchronous receives allow processes to alert the operating system that certain messages are expected and should be delivered to the process as soon as they arrive, even though the process may be busy doing other work at the time. The process does not idly wait for the message to arrive; it continues to execute instructions until the information in the message is required. Then, the process must check its "desktop" to see if the message has, in fact, been delivered. If it has, the process can use it immediately. If the message has not, the process, will, at that point, wait for it to arrive.

A process can also send messages asynchronously. The process alerts the operating system that it wants to send a message, but the process does not wait until the message is sent. This allows it to continue to execute the instructions that follow the send command. This is convenient if a number of messages are being sent, so some messages cannot be sent out immediately. This is similar to placing a document in the FAX queue and resuming work without waiting for the message to be sent.

Interrupt Message Handling. Another way of handling messages in a timely fashion is called *interrupt handling*. Like asynchronous message handling, the process continues working while waiting for the message to arrive. The difference is that with interrupt handling, the process receives an interrupt as soon as the message arrives so it can be processed immediately, rather than having the receiving process post the receive when it is ready to receive it. Afterwards, the process can return to what it was doing when the interrupt occurred.

Lost Messages. A fourth way to handle an incoming document is simply to ignore it because it is not expected or needed. In the parallel programming model, messages directed to the wrong process or to the wrong node are not found and retrieved by the intended process. The node operating system cannot do anything about them because it does not know if another process might later claim them. Such messages remain in system message buffers and thus are "lost."

Cases of lost messages are the result of programming errors and are very difficult to detect without the aid of a debugging tool capable of inspecting system message buffers and unsatisfied requests to receive messages. Fortunately, such debugging tools are usually available.

Performance

Some general terms are used to describe the performance of multiprocessor systems. The two most commonly used terms are *speed-up* and *efficiency*.

Speed-up describes parallel performance as follows:

$$S_p = \frac{T_1}{T_p}$$

Where S_p is speed-up on p nodes, T_1 is the time required using the best sequential algorithm to solve the problem, and T_p is the time required for the parallel algorithm to solve the equation on p nodes. Linear speed-up would mean that the time required to run the problem on one node would be p times the time required to run it on p nodes.

Efficiency is defined as speed-up per node.

$$E_p = \frac{S_p}{p}$$

The performance advantage you get by using a parallel computer over a sequential computer depends upon the type of problem you are solving and the way you have broken the application up into processes (decomposed it). Overhead introduced by the parallel decomposition can adversely affect performance if not done carefully.

For example, you would expect linear speed-up from the kind of problem where the processes running on different nodes are simply different cases of a single program, so concerns about breaking up sequential portions and communication issues do not arise. On the other hand, if you are running a complex single program as a set of processes, it might be more difficult to obtain strictly linear speed-up, although there is no question that the performance would be significantly enhanced.

In the end, the performance of any parallel program depends upon the programmer. The next chapter describes the principles of programming for a loosely-coupled parallel system. Later chapters describe existing decomposition techniques in detail, providing case studies.

3

Working Smart, Not Hard: Parallel Software Engineering Principles

With a programming model in mind, the next step is to understand the process of producing a parallel program. There are three major steps:

1. **Decomposition**—the division of the application into a set of parallel processes and data.

2. **Mapping**—the way processes and data are distributed among the nodes.

3. **Tuning**—alteration of the working application to improve performance.

Inherent in this process are certain principles that are guides to designing an efficient program. These principles help you determine each of the steps of the process:

- Balance the computational load.
- Minimize the communication to computation ratio.
- Reduce sequential bottlenecks.
- Make the program scalable (independent of the actual number of available nodes).

This chapter introduces the program design process, using the calculation of the value of pi as a simple illustration.

Decomposition

The way you decide to "decompose" your application (break it apart into a set of parallel processes and data) must depend on the nature of the algorithm you are using and the structure of the data. Fortunately, you do not have to invent decomposition; a set of decomposition techniques has already been developed.

Because the decomposition step is both the first step and the one that guides the entire programming process, most of the rest of this book is concerned with various decomposition techniques, describing in some detail examples of how these techniques can be applied to various problems. This chapter provides a framework for using these techniques.

The calculation of pi is an example of one of the easiest kinds of problems to decompose, because the decomposition is inherent in the algorithm. This is the standard numerical integration formula for generating pi:

$$\pi = \int_0^1 \frac{4}{1 + x^2} dx$$

A standard method of evaluating this is to divide this area into a number of evenly-spaced strips, and approximate each strip as a rectangle. The value of the function at the midpoint of the strip is taken as the height of the rectangle. The more strips, the more accurate the calculation.

Pi, therefore, is calculated as the sum of the strips in the area under the curve shown in Figure 3.1. This is, in fact, the decomposition of the problem.

A sequential system would simply calculate the area of each rectangle in sequence, and sum the results to produce the answer, as in the following algorithm:

```
input the number n of strips desired
calculate the width w of each strip
for each strip
   find the midpoint x
   compute f(x) and sum
end for
multiply the sum of the heights by the width to get pi
return pi
```

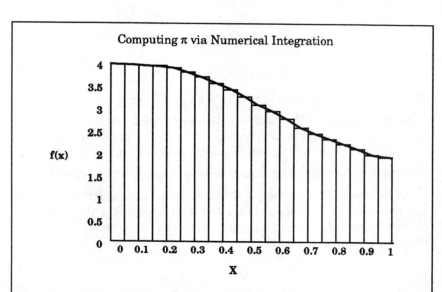

Figure 3.1 Decomposition of the pi calculation.

The following code is a Fortran implementation of this (in the interests of readability, comments are to the right of the code in italics, rather than in the correct Fortran syntax):

```
f(x) = 4.0/(1.0 + x*x)                    define the function
integer n, i
real w, x, sum, pi

read *, n                                 read in the number of strips

w = 1.0/n                                 find the width of each strip

sum = 0.0                                 set sum to 0

do 10 i = 1,n                             for each strip
   x = w*(i-0.5)                          find the midpoint
   sum = sum + f(x)                       calculate the heights and sum
10 continue
```

```
pi = w*sum                                          calculate pi

print *,pi                                            return pi
end
```

The advantages of turning this into a parallel program are clear:

- The calculation of the areas of the rectangles can be distributed among the processors without restricting the order of either the calculation or the summation. This makes it easy to balance the load.

- Communication is required only after the calculation is complete.

Implementing this decomposition on a parallel system therefore requires very little alteration to the sequential code. It is also clear that balancing the load among the processors will not be difficult. This brings up the next step — mapping.

Mapping

Ideally, all nodes dedicated to an application should be busy during the entire time the application is running. While the decomposition of the problem determines whether it will be possible to balance the load for deterministic algorithms, mapping is the step that directly determines the load balance.

When the work load is not equally distributed among the nodes, nodes with smaller loads would sit idle while nodes with the larger work loads continue to process data. The more unequal the loads, the more the computing resources of the system are wasted.

Therefore, it is important in the pi calculation to come up with a way to distribute the calculation of the rectangles equally among the available processors. This is only a matter of dividing up the strips among the available processors. The process assigns rectangles to nodes like dealing out a deck of cards. This ensures that all nodes have an equal (or nearly equal) number of calculations to perform. Figure 3.2 shows this mapping.

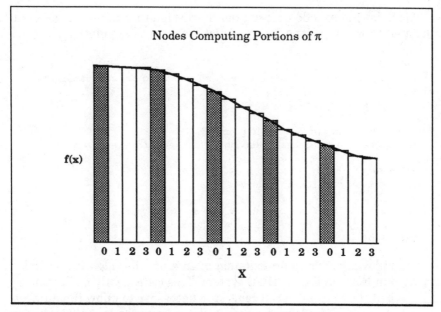

Figure 3.2 Mapping the calculation.

Each node evaluates the function for an assigned set of strips and sums the values for those strips. This leaves certain "managerial" tasks to be done: collecting and summing the partial sums calculated by each node, dividing by the number of strips, and printing the answer. One way to handle this is to use a host system to do it. However, host to node communication is slower than node to node communication, so a better way is to use one node (for example, node 0) to handle these functions. This keeps the load fairly well balanced.

Another of the programming principles is to make the application scalable; that is, to program it so it can be executed independent of how many nodes are currently available to be used. It is generally unwise to design an application for a specific number of nodes. If more than one person is using the computer, the number of available nodes may vary. The size of the system itself may change. Making the application independent of the current number of available nodes makes the software less dependent on the exact configuration of the hardware. Most distributed memory systems offer routines that return the number of nodes in the system, return the node on which a process is executing, and other useful information.

The following pseudo-code defines one design that takes into account the above considerations for a parallel program to calculate pi:

```
if my node is 0
   read the number n of strips desired and send to all other nodes
else
   receive n from node 0
endif
for each strip assigned to this node
   calculate the height of rectangle (at midpoint) and sum result
end for
if my node is not 0
   send sum of results to node 0
else
   receive results from all nodes and sum
   multiply the sum by the width of the strips to get pi
   return pi
```

The following code is an example of this parallel algorithm implemented in Fortran for the iPSC system. This code is only a slight modification of the original serial code. It is necessary to know the number of nodes, and the identifier for each node and process as it executes the code, so there are calls to the **numnodes()**, **mynode()**, and **mypid()** routines to return these, respectively. These statements make it possible to scale the program to run on any number of processors. The if-statements allow node 0 to do the management functions and some of the calculations, while the other nodes perform the bulk of the calculations on their assigned strips and return partial sums to node 0. The **csend** and **crecv** calls are message-passing calls.

```
f(x) = 4.0/(1.0 + x*x)
integer n, i, p, me, mpid
real w, x, sum, pi

p = numnodes()                                    return the number of nodes
me = mynode()                                     return my node's number
mpid = mypid()                                    return my process id
msglen = 4                                        define length of message
allnds = -1                                       define term for all nodes
msgtp0 = 0                                         define term for message type 0
msgtp1 = 1                                         define term for message type 1

if (me .eq. 0) then                               if I am node 0,
   read *, n                                      read the number of strips
   call csend(msgtp0, n, msglen, allnds, mpid)    and send it to all nodes
else                                              If I am any other node
   call crecv(msgtp0, n, msglen)                  receive the value of n
endif

w = 1.0/n
```

```
sum = 0.0

do 10 i = me+1, n, p                         deal out the strips to the processors
   x = w*(i-0.5)
   sum = sum + f(x)
10 continue

if (me .ne. 0) then                                        if I am not node 0
   call csend(msgtp1, sum, 4, 0, mpid)             send my results to node 0
else                                                        if I am node 0
   do 20 i = 1, p-1                          for each of the other processors
      call crecv(msgtp1, temp, 4)              receive the results into temp
      sum = sum + temp                                              and sum
20    continue
   pi = w*sum
   print *,pi
endif

end
```

This implementation functions correctly, balances the load, and is scalable. However, it has a problem. Because all nodes must send their result to node 0, this communication represents a potential bottleneck that could slow down the program. This brings up the next step — tuning.

Tuning

Once an application has been mapped to the nodes of a system and it is running properly, the next step is to tune it to enhance the performance. For the pi calculation, as simple as it is, all that is necessary is to reduce the message bottleneck.

The cost of sending messages between processes is the time required to send and receive them; time that could be spent doing computations that advance the solution of the problem. Therefore, it is important to make the ratio of the number of messages to the number of calculations small to spread the cost of the messages over as many calculations as possible.

For the calculation of pi, having all nodes send messages to node 0 causes a bottleneck at node 0 for two reasons. First, node 0 cannot simultaneously receive more than one message. Second, node 0 must perform the addition on the received information sequentially. By definition, sequential processing is a bottleneck. Some sequential processing is required, but some can be avoided. In this case, a parallel approach is possible.

The software for the iPSC system includes a global summing operation, **gssum**(), for just this kind of problem. The global summing operation iteratively pairs nodes that exchange their current partial sums. Each partial sum received from another node is added to the sum at the receiving node, and this new sum is sent out in the next round of message exchange. Eventually, all of the nodes have accumulated the global sum and node 0 is selected to perform the final multiplication operation and print the result. This global operation can also be programmed manually, but having a set of global operations predefined is both convenient and efficient.

It is important to note that not every node communicates directly with every other node. Information is received second-, third-, or even fourth-hand. In fact, only $\log_2 n$ (where n is the number of nodes) rounds of message exchanges are required, rather than the n messages in the earlier implementation. While there are no fewer messages to be handled, they are now handled in parallel rounds. This parallelism reduces the effective number of messages, enhancing the performance.

To implement this performance enhancement, you would replace this code:

```
if (me .ne. 0) then                          if I am not node 0
   call csend(msgtp1, sum, msglen, 0, mpid)   send my results to node 0
else                                          if I am node 0
   do 20 i = 1, p-1                           for each of the other processors
      call crecv(msgtp1, temp, msglen)        receive the results into temp
      sum = sum + temp                        and sum
20    continue

   pi = w*sum
   print *,pi
endif

end
```

with the following:

```
call gssum(sum, 1, temp)              the parameter 1 indicates a scalar value
if (me .eq. 0) then
   pi = w*sum
   print *, pi
endif
```

Using the global summing routine makes the message-passing more efficient and minimizes the communication to computation ratio.

In other applications, you may find that considerable communication is required directly, but you can "hide" it by using asynchronous message-passing calls and, with processors that implement it, multitasking.

Of course, reducing the communication/computation ratio is not the only tuning issue. The methods available for tuning up the performance of an application are as varied as the kinds of applications, and various performance issues will be explored in later chapters.

The way you initially choose to decompose your application also gives you guidelines for performance tune-ups. The next chapter introduces the standard decomposition techniques.

4

Decomposition Strategies

Producing quality software depends in part upon the approach to the design. To design a sequential program, the first step is to define a very high-level algorithm that outlines how the problem will be solved, and then to define the data structures. This drives the design of the program in detail.

In contrast, in designing a parallel program, the description of the high-level algorithm must include the method you intend to use to break the application into processes and distribute data to different nodes — the *decomposition method*. (Decomposition is distinct from mapping, the physical distribution of the processes among the available nodes.)

The decomposition method you choose drives the rest of the program development. This is true whether you are developing new applications or porting serial code. The decomposition method tells you how to structure the code and data and defines the communication topology. This, in turn, defines the communication protocol.

To choose the best decomposition method for your application, you need to understand your application problem, the data domain, the algorithm(s) used, and the flow of control in your application.

Object-oriented programming, in itself, requires program decomposition, so object-oriented programmers will find parallel programming a natural extension of current practice.

This chapter introduces three general decomposition methods:

- Perfectly parallel decomposition
- Domain decomposition
- Control decomposition

There is also a brief introduction to the object-oriented approach and other techniques for very large applications.

In general, for smaller applications, one of these methods of decomposition will best suit your application and your programming style. For very large applications, you may need to use a combination of these methods.

Perfectly Parallel Application Decomposition

Certain applications fall naturally into the category *perfectly parallel*. Perfectly parallel applications can be divided into a set of processes that require little or no communication with one another. Applications of this kind are usually the easiest to decompose.

The calculation of pi in the previous chapter is a simple example of a perfectly parallel application. The calculation of the areas of the rectangles is divided up among the available processors, and only the results need to be communicated. Further, the order in which the areas of the rectangles are calculated is not important, so no synchronization is required during the calculations.

An obvious way to implement perfect parallelism is simply to run equivalent sequential programs on the various nodes, each with a different data set. On a single processor system, this would require running each case sequentially. While any one instance of the program may run faster on a single larger machine, an entire suite of programs can run on a parallel machine in the same time that it takes to run one. Examples of perfectly parallel applications can be found in most disciplines. Examples from three disciplines are briefly described here: one from chemistry, one from physics and one from finance.

One example of a perfectly parallel application helps chemists determine molecular structure. A standard technique is to calculate the energies of all the possible conformations of a molecule and select the conformation that yields the lowest energy. On a serial machine, this would constitute a systematic iteration through many possible conformations, one at a time. On a parallel machine, each processor can calculate the energies of a subset of the conformations. The calculation would finish with a search for the global minimum.

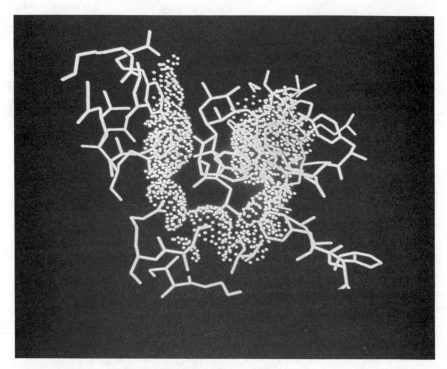

Figure 4.1 Molecular structure simulation.

Real applications of this kind involve modeling proteins with thousands of atoms and millions of possible configurations. On the largest sequential computers, this can take hours or days; a distributed memory parallel system can do the same thing in a fraction of the time.

To determine atomic structure, physicists analyze thousands of random electron distributions around an atomic nucleus to define a probability distribution that points to the probable atomic structure. The Monte Carlo technique is often used to calculate this kind of approximate solution. Monte Carlo calculations typically take a random starting condition for a problem, work through to a solution, save the solution, and start over with another random starting condition. Many iterations of this process allow you to apply standard statistical analysis to the independent solutions to formulate probability curves.

Much like the previous example, each random electron distribution can be calculated independently of the others, making this a perfectly parallel application.

Certain financial problems also lend themselves to perfect parallelism. Frequently, the manager of a large portfolio plays "what if " to determine the best way to distribute investments by subjecting a hypothetical portfolio to predicted market conditions. By modifying the investments several times and reevaluating the portfolio each time, the analyst can determine the most favorable distribution. While this is traditionally done sequentially, on a parallel machine you can run each of the hypothetical cases simultaneously. This is illustrated in Figure 4.2.

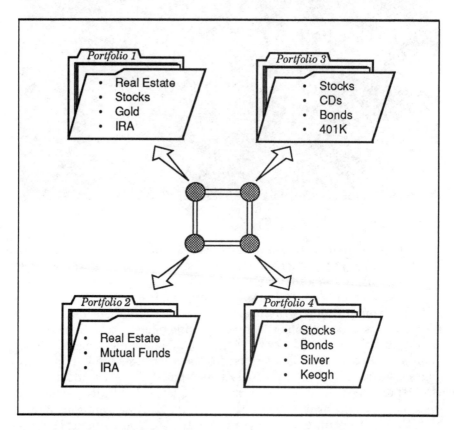

Figure 4.2 Financial portfolio speculation.

Presenting little challenge in terms of computer science or numerical analysis, perfectly parallel applications such as these are nevertheless important applications that demonstrate nearly 100% efficiency (linear speed up) with a minimum of effort. Most distributed-memory parallel systems offer enough memory per node that each process in a perfectly parallel program can be very large and complicated.

Domain Decomposition

Another decomposition technique is called *domain decomposition*. Problems subject to domain decomposition are usually characterized by a large, discrete, static data structure. Decomposing the "domain" of computation, the fundamental data structures, provides the road map for writing the program.

An example of the kind of problem that responds to domain decomposition is a program that simulates aircraft wing stress. Here, the domain is the wing; it is possible to have different processes calculate the stresses for different parts of the wing under given sets of conditions. Figure 4.3 illustrates this.

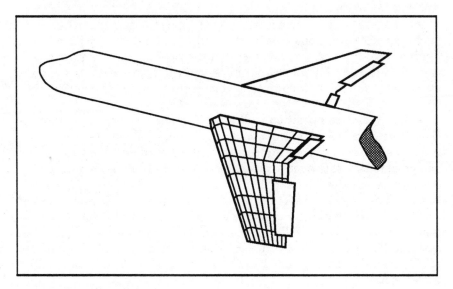

Figure 4.3 Domain decomposition on wing stress simulation.

Domain decomposition works particularly well for the following three kinds of problems:

- Problems where the data is static. For example, factoring and solving a large matrix or finite difference calculations on a mesh are both natural candidates for domain decomposition.

- Problems where the data structure is dynamic, but it is tied somehow to a single entity. For example, in a large multi-body problem, some subset of the bodies could be distributed to each node. Even though the bodies might be moving through space and interacting with each other, the calculations for each body can stay on the original node.

• Problems where the domain is fixed but the computation within various regions of the domain is dynamic. An example of this kind of application is a program that models fluid vortices, where the domain (say, a section of the Gulf Stream) stays fixed but the whirlpools move around.

The next chapter discusses the principles of domain decomposition and provides more detailed examples.

Control Decomposition

Another major decomposition strategy is called *control decomposition*. When there is no static structure or fixed determination of the numbers of objects or calculations to be performed, domain decomposition is not appropriate. Instead, you can focus on the flow of control in the application. As the development progresses, you will also distribute the data structures, but the guideline to development remains the flow of control.

One control decomposition technique is called functional decomposition. Here, you look at a problem as a set of operations (in terms of its functions), defining your processes based on those operations. For example, to simulate a large mechanical system, such as a power plant, it might be most efficient to define the processes in terms of the functions of the parts of the system. One process might simulate the cooling system, one the generator, another the heat exchanger. A natural communications scenario follows the physical coupling of these subsystems. The granularity of the solution would depend on the number of processors in the system and the amount of work associated with each function.

Another control decomposition technique is called *manager/worker*. This technique uses one process as the "manager", which farms out the tasks (processes) to each of the "workers" (nodes) and keeps track of the progress of the computation as the workers report back with completed tasks. A simple application of this technique is the construction of a frame buffer in an image processing application. The manager sends sub-portions of the image to the workers, who massage the data and return it. However, some portions of the image may require more computation than others, making it most efficient to use a manager to send the next piece of work to the next available worker, rather than predefining the distribution in the program.

Chapter 6 deals with control decomposition in more detail.

Object-Oriented Programming

Object-oriented programming provides another approach to program decomposition. Object-oriented programmers view applications as a set of abstract data structures, or objects. Associated with these objects are tasks, so there is no confusion about the parts of the code and data that affect other parts.

It is possible, therefore, to view object oriented programming as a formalization of domain and/or control decomposition, because both data and functions must be considered to create objects. If you take an object-oriented approach to programming, you already think in terms that will help you design programs for distributed-memory parallel systems.

Problems that involve scheduling, such as air traffic or port management, lend themselves particularly well to this approach. Each plane or ship, could, for example, be modeled as an object with individual behavior; simulation and management of these objects could then be allocated among the available nodes.

Object-oriented programming for parallel systems is described in more detail in Chapter 7.

Decomposition Methods for Very Large Applications

No single decomposition technique may be quite what you need for very large and complex applications. You may need to view the application as a set of layers, and apply different decomposition methods to different layers of the problem. This is referred to as *layered decomposition*.

Chapter 6 contains a brief description of an application to which layered decomposition is applied.

5

Domain Decomposition:
Examples and Techniques

The main characteristic of many applications is regularity in the domain or data structures. Domain decomposition was developed to make problems of this kind easy to translate to a parallel system. Second to perfectly parallel decomposition, domain decomposition is, in fact, the most straightforward of the decomposition techniques.

The general approach to the domain decomposition of an application is as follows:

1. Distribute the domain.

2. Restrict the computation so that each process updates its own data.

3. Put in the communication

This chapter offers four examples of applications that are subject to domain decomposition:

* Matrix factoring
* Seismic modeling
* Finite element problems
* Two-dimensional Fast Fourier Transform (FFT)

Porting Techniques

Frequently, it is necessary to port sequential programs to a parallel system. If these programs have a regular domain, they are candidates for domain decomposition. Naturally, before you start, you need to decide how to approach the distribution of data.

An efficient porting procedure is as follows:

1. Compile and test an existing serial program on one node. This allows you to resolve any compiler and I/O problems before complications arise.

2. Run multiple copies of the program at once.

3. Put in the communication; run on all nodes. This allows you to debug the communication.

4. Restrict the computation so that each node updates its own data; run the program.

5. Restrict the data; run the program.

6. Tune the program to enhance the performance.

The advantage of this approach is that the effects of each step are localized. This usually helps to reduce the debugging effort.

Matrix Factoring

Porting code to a distributed-memory parallel system can be a relatively simple task, as experience has shown. In many cases, you need to add only a few lines of code, using simple system calls to express the inherent parallelism of the application. The example in this section is of that kind -- originally coded for a sequential system, and easily ported to a parallel system.

In fact, there are several very good reasons for trying to use existing sequential algorithms:

1. You already understand the algorithms.

2. The algorithm's performance is well-known.

3. Algorithms such as those in LINPACK are known to exhibit high accuracy with varied input data.

4. It is usually ill-advised to reinvent a solution when a satisfactory solution exists.

One of the well-known algorithms in the LINPACK linear equations package is the Gaussian elimination algorithm for factoring a square matrix into lower and upper triangular factors. The regular nature of the algorithm makes it inherently parallel, and the regularity of the domain makes it easy to distribute. It is, therefore, an obvious candidate for domain decomposition. Distributing the domain requires only that the matrix be divided into sections, and distributing the sections among the processors.

You can implement the distribution of the data with only a small change to the existing code. The distributed algorithm solves the problem in parallel on all of the available processors, making it possible to solve much larger problems than could be considered on a single processor. When the problem is large, it can be solved with a speed proportional to the number of processors.

The Sequential Gaussian Elimination Algorithm

The Gaussian elimination algorithm for factoring a square matrix into lower and upper triangular factors is a triply-nested loop. The outer loop controls how much of the matrix remains to be factored. At each iteration, the remaining part of the matrix to be factored is a smaller square submatrix in the lower right-hand corner of the original matrix. A major characteristic of this application is that it requires that information from one node be broadcast to all other nodes.

The code implements these steps:

1. Choose a pivot element from the first column of the submatrix.

2. Swap the pivot row with the first row.

3. Divide the pivot column by the pivot.

4. Subtract the pivot column, appropriately scaled, from each remaining column.

The sequential algorithm is as follows:

```
for i = 1, ..., N-1 do
    Find the index ip of the maximal element of the portion of the
        i^th column of A below the diagonal
    Swap rows of i and ip of A
    Divide the pivot column, A_{i+1i} through A_{Ni}, by the pivot A_{ii}
    Scale and subtract the pivot column from each remaining column
end for
```

This algorithm is coded in Fortran as part of LINPACK, and is called "dgefa" (double precision general factor). It can be executed directly on a single node of a parallel system, completing the first step of the porting process.

Determining the Matrix Distribution

The next step is to decide how to distribute the matrix. (Coding the matrix distribution comes later in the porting process.) The matrix is a regular data structure, making it easy to distribute it among the processors by columns. There are three reasons to divide it into columns rather than rows:

1. In the code being ported (the LINPACK version), dgefa is implemented by columns.
2. By partitioning the matrix into columns, the vectors are long, giving better performance on a vector machine.

The sequential algorithm operates on smaller and smaller submatrices at each step of the outer loop, so you map the domain to the processors in such a way that all processors own approximately the same number of columns of the submatrix. If the number of columns is evenly divisible by the number of processors, then all processors own exactly the same number of columns; otherwise some processors own one more column.

Two common ways to map the columns are *block mapping* and *column-wrapped mapping*. With the block mapping technique, you divide the columns into a set of blocks, and distribute a block to each processor. With column-wrapped mapping, you deal out the columns to the processors like dealing out cards to several players, as illustrated in Figure 5.1.

Column-wrapped mapping runs 30-50% faster than block mapping in this case. This is because after a column has been the pivot column, it requires no further computation. Further, this operation proceeds from the first column to the last, sequentially. (Imagine it starting in the first column of Figure 5.1 and moving right, one column at a time.) Therefore, if you mapped the columns to the processors as blocks, the first processor would finish its work and be idle, then the second, etc., until the last processor finished its work, as illustrated in Figure 5.2.

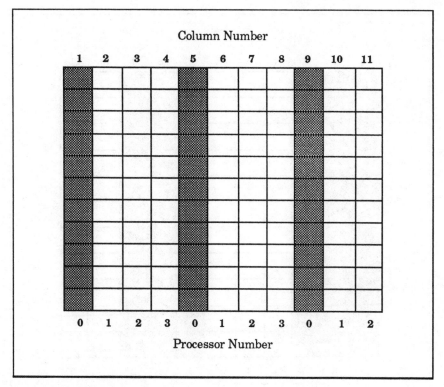

Figure 5.1 Column-wrapped mapping of a matrix.

However, by using column-wrapped mapping, all processors can be working during most of the computation.

Distributing the Computation

Once you decide how to distribute the domain, the next step is to modify the algorithm to distribute the computation. Using column-wrapped mapping in distributing the data, a new processor owns the pivot column at each step. This makes it reasonable to design the parallel algorithm so the processor that owns the pivot column controls the computation at that step.

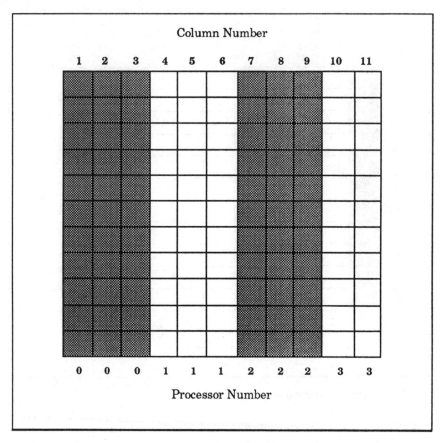

Figure 5.2 Block mapping.

The calculation starts, therefore, with the processor owning the first column finding the pivot element, swaps the pivot row with the first row, and divides the pivot column by the pivot, just as in the serial algorithm. After this computation, the processor then broadcasts the pivot column and the pivot row number as a message to all the other processors. No further computation is then required on the pivot column.

When another processor receives this message, it swaps its pivot row with its first row. By this means, all of the processors, including the owner of the pivot column, subtract the pivot column, appropriately scaled, from each remaining column.

In the parallel algorithm below, the number of processors is p, and the index of the processor is me. The value of me is different for each processor and is in the range $0 \le$ me $<$ p. Aside from that, each processor uses the same algorithm. The parallel algorithm, therefore, is as follows:

```
me <- index of processor
for i = 1, ..., N-1 do
  if (i-1 mod p) = me then
    Find the index ip of the maximal element of the i^th column of A
    Swap rows of i and ip of A, so A_ii is the pivot element.

    Divide the pivot column, A_{i+1i} through A_Ni, by the pivot A_ii

    Broadcast the pivot column, A_{i+1i} through A_Ni, and the row number
ip to swap
  else
    Receive the pivot column and the pivot row number.
    Swap rows i and ip.
  endif
  Scale and subtract the pivot column from each remaining column
end for
```

The original serial algorithm is altered only by the addition of a test to see which processor owns the pivot column, and system calls to send the pivot information to the other processors. In fact, when executed on a single processor, it is reduced to the standard Gaussian elimination algorithm.

This simple change results in an efficient parallel algorithm; for large matrices, it runs with a speed proportional to the number of processors. This efficiency is possible because of the column-wrapped mapping, a straightforward and effective method of distributing the columns of the matrix (the domain) among the processors.

Tuning Issues

As described earlier, column-wrapped mapping of the matrix results in some performance improvement. You can improve the performance even more if you "hide" the sequential nature of pivoting. In general, the algorithm is essentially sequential; while the pivot column is pivoting, all of the other processes are waiting for it. When the pivot is finally broadcast, the other processes all subtract; then the next node pivots, etc.

To improve the efficiency, it is important to remember that each processor owns several columns. This means that as soon as the first column broadcasts the pivot, all processors except the one owning the next pivot subtract the pivot column from all of the columns. The processor owning the second column, however, does only the subtraction on the column that will be the pivot, which it then pivots and broadcasts. Then it can continue subtracting the first pivot column from all of its other columns, while the processor owning the third column subtracts, pivots, and broadcasts. In this way, more of the processors can be busy more of the time, improving the efficiency.

Seismic Modeling

Another example that illustrates the domain decomposition technique is seismic simulation. A standard technique for locating natural fuel reserves is to develop a model of the location and composition of the earth's strata (layers). This is an iterative process, with seismic simulation a computationally demanding step. Previously, large mainframe vector computers have been required to carry out the simulation. This section describes the problem and its parallel implementation. Figure 5.3 illustrates the general concept.

The first step in the seismic simulation process is to obtain field data in the area of interest. A series of explosions (seismic events) are set off near the surface of the earth, and the ground motion over time is recorded at points in a line along the surface.

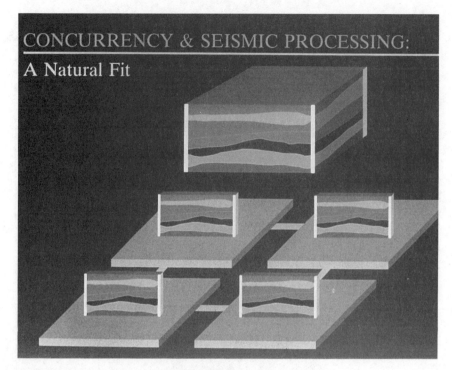

Figure 5.3 Concurrency and seismic processing.

The seismic simulation starts with an initial model of the distribution of strata. Each type of stratum is characterized by the density and velocity of the waves traveling through it. The wave equation is used to simulate the reflection of the seismic waves resulting from the explosion. At each iteration, the simulation results are compared to the field data from the area of interest. The depth and composition of the strata are adjusted to approach the field results.

These steps are repeated until the simulation accurately reproduces the arrival time, amplitude, and phase of reflected waves in the data. When this is true, the model reflects the actual depth and composition of each of the strata.

The model used is a two-dimensional rectangle. This is mainly because the field data against which the model is compared consist of a time series along a single line. Thus, there is no gain in using a three-dimensional model.

This two-dimensional rectangle is defined at the top corner by the location of the explosion, and arbitrary points at some distance into the earth and along the surface of the earth from the point of the explosion, as indicated in Figure 5.4.

To make sure the model is as accurate as possible, it is important to set realistic boundary conditions.

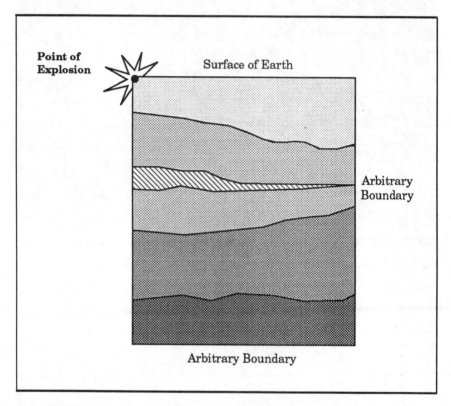

Figure 5.4 Setting the boundaries of the seismic calculation.

The boundary defined by the surface of the earth is a reflecting boundary. Like the surface of a drum, it both reacts to the stimulus and reflects the waves that strike it. The vertical boundary at the source of seismic energy is assumed to be symmetrical; that is, whatever occurs within the rectangle of interest is assumed to occur in a similar rectangle on the other side of that boundary. Neither the reflecting nor the symmetrical boundary conditions require significantly more calculation, and so are not of major concern in the distribution of the domain.

The other two boundaries are defined to be nonreflecting (absorbing) boundaries, because the waves should continue on as they reach those boundaries. The non-reflecting boundary conditions are more complex and require more calculating time.

You can now visualize the model as shown in Figure 5.5.

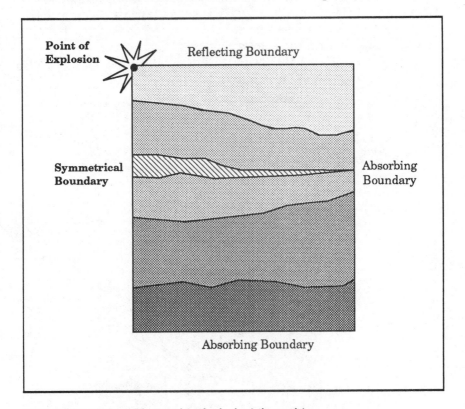

Figure 5.5 Boundary conditions on the seismic simulation model.

Distributing the Domain

One of the characteristics of this application is that it is a "local" computation. Calculating the updated pressure at each point in the domain requires only the information of the points immediately surrounding it. When you divide the domain among processors, each sub-domain must exchange the points at its edge for the points at the edge of its immediate neighbor. The communication remains localized; there is no need to broadcast information globally, as was required in the matrix factoring application.

There are two common ways to distribute the domain. One is to divide it into vertical strips, and the other into squares. There are advantages to both methods. Dividing it into vertical strips provides very long vectors, while squares give you a better communication-to-computation ratio due to their smaller perimeter. In this example, the domain is partitioned as a set of vertical strips, because the implementation of this problem (see Appendix A) was on a vector system, on which this distribution funs faster.

Figure 5.6 illustrates the model with the domain decomposed into vertical strips for execution on a parallel system.

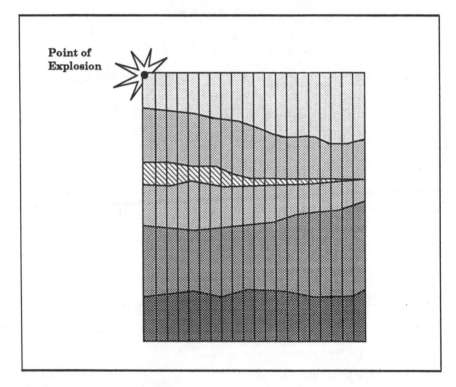

Figure 5.6 Decomposing the domain.

The Serial Algorithm

The technique used to solve the problem is to update the vectors v (representing the displacement of the earth at the previous time step) in terms of u (displacement at the current time step) and c (the scaled square of the speed of sound) using centered second-order differences. The process is repeated for each time step.

At each time step, the serial algorithm used to solve the seismic simulation problem can be described as follows:

```
Save boundary values of u for use in the absorbing boundary condition.
Update v in the interior using u and c.
Update the boundary values of v.
The next step is to swap u and v logically, and repeat for the next
   time step.
```

Defining the Parallel Algorithm

On a distributed-memory system with p nodes, the arrays u and c are distributed over the processors, so each processor owns a strip of each of these arrays, corresponding to a vertical strip of the model. If the number of gridlines is divisible by the number of nodes, each node could be assigned a strip of the same width. However, in general, some nodes will have one extra gridline.

As mentioned earlier, each node computes and updates the positions of the points within the interior of the strip assigned to it. However, to compute updated values at points on its first gridline (the leading edge of the strip), each node needs values of u on the last gridline of the previous strip, which belongs to another node. Similarly, to compute the values of points on its last gridline, each node needs the values of u for the first gridline of the next strip. These points belonging to another processor are called "ghost points".

At the beginning of each time step, each node must send the values of u on its first and last gridline to the nodes that own the neighboring strips and receive values of u from these nodes. To accommodate this, the array containing u on each node is declared large enough to hold one gridline of each adjacent strip. This produces the following parallel algorithm:

```
Trade edges of the strip with the adjacent processors (send boundary
    gridline, wait for gridline from adjacent strips).
If appropriate, save true boundary values (for absorbing boundary
    condition).
Update my part of v.
Update the boundary values.
```

Tuning Issues

For this problem, the factors that most affect the performance, in general, are the overhead associated with communication and the load balance among the available processors.

To reduce the communication overhead, you can alter the algorithm to compute the interior values of v before the values of u for points on the edges of the strip are received from the adjacent nodes. While the processor is computing the interior points, the communications network trades the edges of the strip with the adjacent nodes. When the communication is finished, the edges of the strip can be computed. This more efficient algorithm could be expressed as follows:

```
Set up to receive ghost points from the processor on the left.
Set up to receive ghost points from the processor on the right.
Start sending ghost points to the processor on the left.
Start sending ghost points to the processor on the right.
Update interior of v
Wait for completion of the message from the processor on left.
Wait for completion of the message from the processor on right.
Update boundary values
```

This permits the communication and computation to overlap completely, so the details of message overhead or bandwidth do not affect the performance of the algorithm. It remains only to ensure that the communication bandwidth is sufficient to finish sending and receiving each message before the data in the message is needed for computation. This algorithm is designed to be sufficiently coarse-grained to optimize performance.

The other factor, as always, is the effect of the balance of the load on the efficiency of the algorithm. If one node must wait too long for another node to send its data, the load is not perfectly balanced. In this example, there are two issues that might cause an imbalance in the load:

1. Some nodes may own one more line of the grid than other nodes own.

2. The two nodes owning the vertical edges of the rectangle have the additional work of computing the boundary conditions.

As it turns out, the extra grid line allotted to some nodes has a very small affect on the balance of the load. Symmetric boundary conditions are relatively inexpensive to calculate, so the extra work of the node owning the left-most gridline also has no major unbalancing effect. In addition, the absorbing boundary on the bottom is distributed among the nodes.

However, the node that owns the extreme right strip must calculate the non-reflecting boundary condition. The non-reflecting boundary condition, as implemented, takes as long as updating several lines of the interior. The simple solution is to assign fewer gridlines to the node that owns the non-reflecting right boundary condition than to the other nodes. The result is a fairly balanced load that does not adversely affect performance.

The Fortran code for this application is in Appendix A.

The Finite Element Method

The finite element method is a widely-used traditional technique for solving real-world problems on sequential computer systems. The solution of partial differential equations in two or three dimensions is one class of problem solved with this method. Problems of this kind occur in a range of fields that includes structures, fluids, electromagnetics, and integrated circuit modeling. Domain decomposition works to parallelize problems of this kind.

The problem region is divided into a large number of subdomains (the *finite elements*), and separate calculations are performed on each subdomain. The solution to the original problem is approximated by fitting together functions defined within each piece. The use of this technique precedes not only parallel computers, but computers themselves, when the "elements" were identical to actual structural members and the calculations were done by hand.

The finite element method is in itself a type of domain decomposition. As described earlier, decomposition and mapping are the two steps that allow you to implement algorithms on parallel computers. The basic idea is to break the problem up (decomposition) and assign the pieces to the nodes (mapping). Defining the finite elements is the decomposition step, dividing the problem region into domains. It only remains to map the elements to the processors and then balance the load and the communication-to-computation ratio, as described earlier.

A typical use for the finite element method is the solution of a partial differential equation defined over some problem region in two or three dimensions. First, some approximating function is found that solves the partial differential equation. Then, the problem region is split into pieces. Some simple form for the approximating function is assumed in each piece (e.g., piecewise linear polynomials). Figure 5.7 shows a region R subdivided into elements.

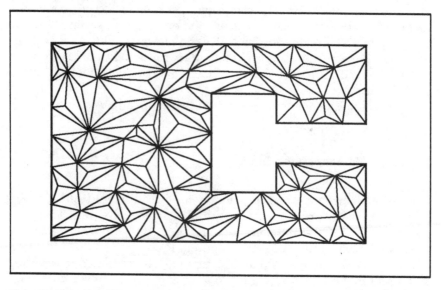

Figure 5.7 The region "R" subdivided into elements.

Next, define an approximation to the desired function piecewise over the problem region. Substituting this approximation into the expression for the function, and minimizing the result with respect to the unknown parameters produces a matrix equation. The integrals are evaluated separately over each element, and the results added to form the global matrix.

This assembly phase of the finite element method typically consumes from 25% to 50% of the total computing time. Most of the rest of the time is consumed in the linear equation phase (the matrix factoring example earlier in this chapter describes a method for linear equation manipulation in parallel). Because the assembly phase involves a major portion of the overall processor time, it is a good candidate for a parallel implementation.

The Sequential Algorithm

In the assembly process, a very large number of integrals must be evaluated. The amount of work per element will depend on the particular element type and will often involve expensive numerical integration. Figure 5.8 is a flow chart of the sequential assembly algorithm.

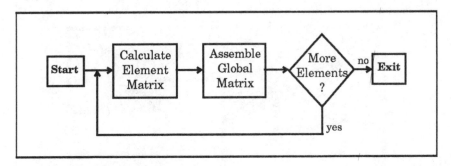

Figure 5.8 Sequential assembly algorithm.

The Parallel Algorithm

Dividing the problem region R into elements is the decomposition of the problem. The mapping consists of assigning the elements to the individual processors. You can do this either arbitrarily or according to some specific pattern. The simplest mapping involves dividing the set of elements into p groups (where p is the number of available processors), each containing nearly the same number of elements, and assigning each group to one of the processors. This balance of elements between the processors usually results in good load balance for the parallel algorithm because the time required to solve each region is approximately equal.

Figure 5.9 shows a mapping of the element groups to sixteen processors.

In addition to decomposing the elements, you must divide up the unknowns so that the global equation for each unknown resides on a specified processor. If there are n global unknowns, you can assign the first n/p to the first processor, the next n/p to the second, and so on. If p does not divide n evenly, some processors may get one extra unknown.

Figure 5.9 Mapping the elements to sixteen processors.

The assembly process requires two steps: element matrix generation and global matrix assembly. In the sequential algorithm, each element matrix is assembled into the global matrix as soon as it is calculated. In contrast, in the parallel algorithm, one processor may be calculating entries that belong to the global equation of another processor. This requires, therefore, some communication among the processors.

Then, you would modify the algorithm shown in Figure 5.7 so that after an element matrix has been computed, the information is sent to each processor that owns any of the unknowns for that element. In its turn, the routine must receive messages from other processors as contributions to its rows come in. This produces the parallel assembly algorithm shown in Figure 5.10.

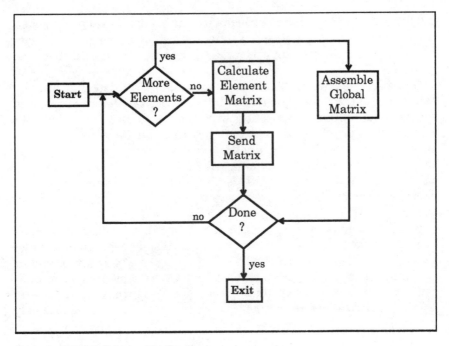

Figure 5.10 The parallel assembly algorithm.

Tuning Issues

Load balance and communication can be adjusted to improve the performance of finite element problems.

As suggested earlier, nearly equal numbers of elements are assigned to each processor. Provided that the work involved in calculating the element matrices is equal (as it generally is for a given type of element), the load is well-balanced. Poor load balance can only arise if the number of elements is not much greater than the number of processors.

The communication issue is more interesting. The flow chart for the parallel algorithm shows messages being sent out after each element matrix calculation. Of course, if the processor that has done the element matrix calculation owns some or all of the unknowns whose equations have been computed, it need not send a message and can proceed directly with the global assembly step.

This presents a genuine performance-tuning opportunity. By sensibly numbering the unknowns, you can select a mapping of elements that minimizes the amount of communication that must occur between processors.

Going further, you could eliminate this communication altogether by taking the set of unknowns owned by a given processor and assigning all elements containing any of those unknowns to that processor. With this scheme, all of the information generated in the element matrix computation could be used locally, and no communication would be necessary. The price you would pay for this improvement in the communication-to-computation ratio is that some of the elements would be assigned to more than one processor and redundant computation would occur.

In general, however, experience has shown that in systems such as the iPSC systems, the communication is fast enough that parallel assembly is highly efficient without resorting to any renumbering or assigning elements to multiple processors. In the same vein, other tuning techniques such as combining messages (e.g., calculating several element matrices before communicating) are possible but are probably unnecessary.

Two Dimensional Complex FFTs

Many image- and signal-processing applications require the computation of multidimensional Fast Fourier Transforms (FFT). The simplest algorithm for computing a two-dimensional FFT is to compute a one-dimensional FFT on each row of the data followed by one-dimensional FFTs on each column.

You can take advantage of vector processors and their corresponding vector software routines by storing entire rows or columns on one node. This means that you should partition the matrix either by rows or by columns. As it turns out, partitioning into rows is slightly better for communication.

For example, consider a 32x32 problem on four vector nodes. Each node will contain an 8x32 slice of the problem, so each node can do eight FFTs of rows of length 32, in parallel with the other three nodes, as shown in Figure 5.11.

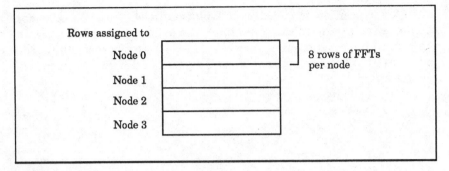

Figure 5.11 Distributing the FFT data among the nodes.

Then, before the column FFTs can be computed, it is necessary to transpose the matrix. During the transpose phase, each of the nodes has a different 8x8 square of complex numbers that must be sent to each of the other nodes. By slicing the global data structure by rows, these squares are sequential in memory and can be sent directly without having to copy them to a buffer. In addition, each of the squares must be transposed locally. Figure 5.12 shows how the data would be distributed and the destination node of each square.

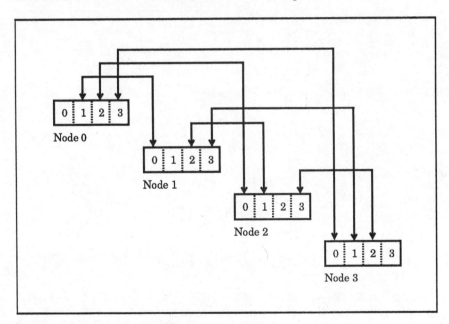

Figure 5.12 Transposing the FFT data among the nodes.

The transposition is coded in p-1 phases in which pairs of nodes exchange their data. In the first phase, the pairs are (0,1) and (2,3). In the second phase, the pairs are (0,2) and (1,3). In the last phase, the pairs are (0,3) and (1,2). The following algorithm describes this implementation:

```
p = numnodes()
for i = 1 to p do
    dest = xor(mynode(), i)
    send data block to dest
    receive data block from dest
    do local transpose of received block
end for
do local transposition of diagonal block
```

The result of using the sequencing described in this algorithm is that there is no contention in the message-passing network. All of the messages in each of the phases can be sent simultaneously. This algorithm does, in fact, work without contention for any number of nodes.

The Fortran code for this application is in Appendix A.

Control Decomposition: Examples and Techniques

Domain decomposition relies on some regularity in the domain and/or data structures of an application, so not all applications can be decomposed efficiently with this method. When the domain and data structures are irregular or unpredictable, you need to resort to other methods of organizing the parallel decomposition.

One approach is to focus on distributing the flow of control of the computation rather than distributing the domain. The collection of techniques based on this approach is called *control decomposition*. You will also have to distribute the domain during the program development, but, unlike domain decomposition, the guideline of the development is not the domain, but the control aspects.

An example of a domain that is not amenable to domain decomposition is the search space created by a game tree, where the branching factor varies from node to node. Any static assignment of the tree is either impossible or leads to a poorly balanced load.

Because many symbolic applications tend to have irregular structures, control decomposition is often associated with artificial intelligence (AI) and other non-numeric applications. However, control decomposition techniques (like domain decomposition techniques) are important for both symbolic and numeric applications. It is important to bear in mind that the approach you choose should not be based solely on whether the application is symbolic or numeric, but on the regularity and/or predictability of the main data structures. Choosing the right decomposition approach for the parallel program has an impact both on performance (because of the effect on the load balance and the communication/computation ratio) and on how easy the program is to write and maintain.

There are several approaches to implementing control decomposition. This chapter describes the two most common techniques, which have been used for most of the known applications that are not domain decompositions:

- Functional control
- Manager/worker control

The next section of this chapter looks briefly at image processing as an example of one kind of functional decomposition. Following this is a discussion of the manager/worker approach to an application that performs a design rule check of integrated circuits. Finally, the triangle game is used as a relatively simple example of a problem that is best parallelized using the manager/worker control decomposition method.

Functional Decomposition

It is natural to look at any algorithm as a set of modules that express the functional parts of the algorithm. This is a kind of decomposition that is often depicted as a diagram such as the one in Figure 6.1.

The Manager/Worker Approach to Design Rule Checking

One application for which the manager/worker approach works well is a design rule checker for semiconductor device designs. Design rules define the restrictions on laying out the physical device (how far apart connecting paths must be, restrictions in the angles of turns, etc.). After the device is designed and laid out electronically, the design rule check makes sure all of the design rules have been satisfied. Typically, this requires a lot of processing. One approach to making this a parallel application is to use domain decomposition to divide the chip into rectangular pieces and assign processes to each one of the pieces, as illustrated in Figure 6.2.

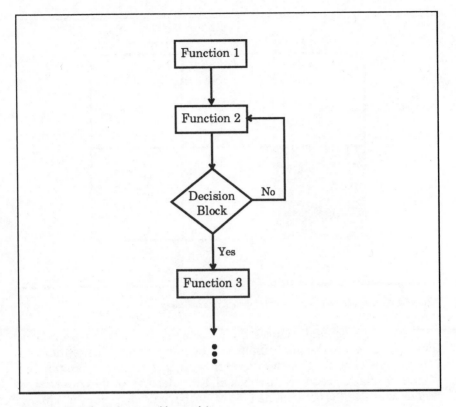

Figure 6.1 Functional decomposition model.

The amount of work to be done in each section, however, is directly dependent upon the amount of artwork within each one of the squares, and therefore varies greatly from square to square. In practice it has been found to be more efficient to divide the initial design rule problem into squares, and then have a manager hand out the squares to the workers as they become available. This takes advantage of the dynamic load balancing inherent in manager/worker. Experience has shown that having at least four times as many problems as workers permits a good load balance.

Two kinds of communication are necessary. The first is the standard communication between the manager and the worker, and the second is communication between processes concerning geometries just outside a given square. This communication is rather complex and could be time-consuming because a given process doesn't know which workers, if any, currently own the squares bordering its square.

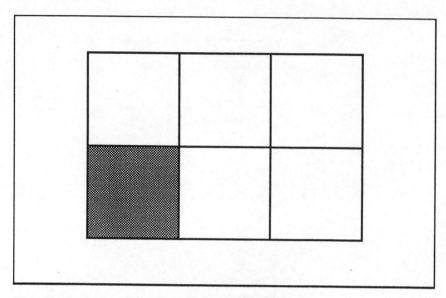

Figure 6.2 Domain decomposition of IC for design rule checking.

A simple refinement reduces the complexity of this communication, thereby improving the performance of the application. This refinement is to include enough of the border area with each square to provide the extra information required to check all the rules within the square. The border area itself is not included in the design rule check for the square. Figure 6.3 illustrates this solution.

The Triangle Problem

The combinatorial problem is another type of application for which the manager/worker approach provides an efficient solution. This section describes in detail a problem of this type: the "triangle" problem. This is represented by a game in which the board has a triangle shape with 15 holes. Initially, there is a peg in all holes but the central one, as shown in Figure 6.4.

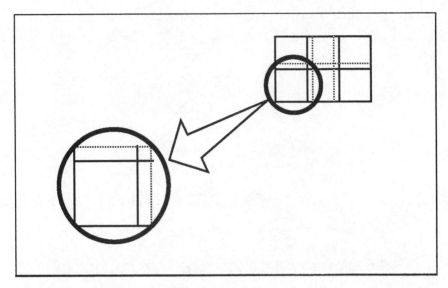

Figure 6.3 Performance enhancement for the design rule check.

The game is a series of moves where you jump a peg over another peg into an unoccupied hole, removing the peg you jumped over. The object is to leave a single peg on the board. The problem for the computer is to find all of the correct solutions. This requires a search through all of the possible sequences of moves (given the position of the initial hole) to find all possible solutions.

The manager/worker approach is well-suited to problems of this type. There is no way to predict how much computation will result from any given search path, so simply dividing up the domain among the processors would be likely to result in an unbalanced load — some processors becoming quickly idle while others are overloaded.

The Sequential Algorithm. The initial set-up of the board allows a single hole without a peg (the standard set-up puts the hole in the center of the board, as shown in Figure 6.4). The sequential algorithm for solving the problem uses a depth-first search pattern, following each search path until no further moves are possible, either because a solution is found, or it has reached a dead end. When a path reaches an endpoint, the algorithm backtracks until a branch produces a new path. This algorithm is outlined as follows:

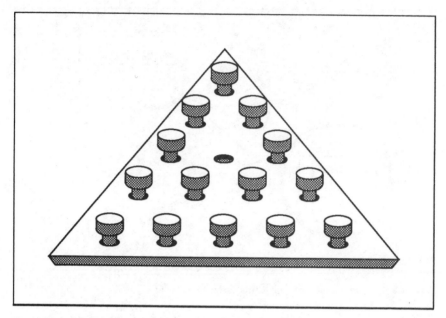

Figure 6.4 The triangle game board.

```
Initialize board Call depth_first_search(1)                    top level call
/* list solutions here */
exit();

depth_first_search(depth)
{

   If depth = 14 {
   store solution
   }
else{ for each possible move from this board position
   {
     change board to show move
     store move in sequence
     call depth_first_search(depth+1)
     unmake move, remove last move from sequence[]
   }
return
}
```

The Parallel Algorithm. The parallel solution resolves itself into one algorithm for the manager, and one for the workers. The manager creates the top level of the search tree by solving a fixed number of moves (for example, down to a depth of four) to create enough subproblems on the search tree for an efficient solution. The manager then distributes nodes to the workers as they become available. Each worker then finds all of the solutions for the branching that each has been given.

The ratio of the number of expanded nodes to the number of available processors has been determined generally to fall in the range between four and ten. That is, there should be from four to ten times as many unsolved problems as there are workers. The higher the number of unsolved problems, the more likely it is that there will be an even load balance, but it is best not to reduce the granularity to the point that more time is required for communication than computation.

Because the triangle problem involves a relatively small number of total moves (a maximum of 14 for a successful solution), only the manager is required to create the nodes of the search tree initially. However, in larger, more complex problems of this type on systems with a large number of nodes, it may be inefficient for a single manager to produce enough nodes for the number of workers available because the manager could become the bottleneck. For problems like this, the manager can hand nodes out to the submanagers, and ask them to build the next level on the search tree and return that level to the manager. The manager then glues those into the search tree, records the number of new problems, and so forth until there is a large enough ratio of problems for the number of workers.

For the triangle problem, the worker need only respond to a "solve" request — to take the position handed to it and find all possible solutions. The manager must expand the first few levels, keep track of the unexpanded nodes to be sent to the workers, send problems to workers as they become available, and receive results. Figure 6.5 shows the host and node algorithms for the triangle problem on a parallel system.

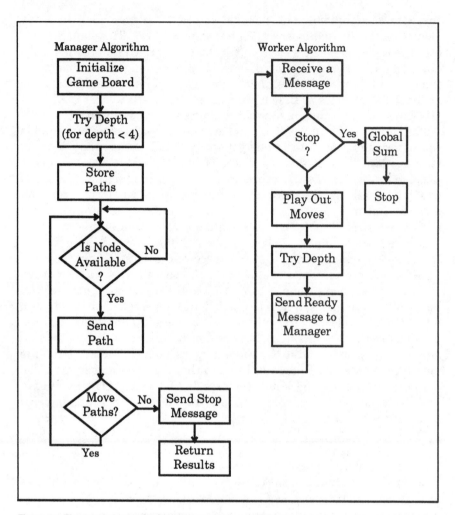

Figure 6.5 The parallel triangle manager and worker algorithms.

Performance Tuning

There are several techniques for tuning the performance when you use the manager/worker approach to decomposition. One technique is to double-buffer messages. The idea is to send a worker two pieces of information (two pieces of work) the first time. The worker code is unchanged. Only the system software on the node realizes there are two messages waiting.

The result of double-buffering messages is that as soon as the worker is finished working on the first one, another piece of work is immediately available. It is not necessary to wait for the manager to supply new information. If the communication/computation issues have been well-balanced, the original results of the first piece of work would go back to the manager, who can respond with another piece of work before the worker finishes the second piece.

From this point on, there is always one problem waiting in the worker's queue, and the manager returns a new problem every time the worker returns a solution.

Another issue is that the manager can become the bottleneck because it is maintaining a global data structure and the list of work being done by the workers. Experience has shown that with up to 50 workers and a good communication/computation ratio, the manager is very rarely the bottleneck. In fact, because the amount of work in each problem varies, it is unlikely that two workers will respond to the manager at the same time. Therefore the irregularity is actually an advantage to the manager/worker paradigm. If the problems require the same amount of work, it actually creates more of a bottleneck and causes more problems than it solves.

However, for the thousands of processors and thousands of workers of machines in the near future, a single manager clearly can become the bottleneck. The solution, of course, is to go to a second layer of management. This would mean a manager of managers and then several managers, each of which has several workers associated with it. One form of this has been implemented by Feldman Otto in a chess playing program.

The final performance consideration might be to have both a worker process and the manager process on the same processor (for multitasking processors). If the manager seems to be idle most of the time, this would allow the recapture of the idle time for the manager. However, this should be done only after careful consideration, because if the worker process is running on the manager processor when a message for the manager comes, it can cause significant delay responding to workers, resulting in degradation of the overall system performance.

Large-Scale Decomposition Techniques

Some problems, especially large and complex problems, do not lend themselves to a single approach to decomposition. A pragmatic approach to a problem of this kind is to use the layered decomposition approach.

At its most basic level, the image processing application described earlier can be seen as an example of a two-layered decomposition. At the top level, it is a large-grained pipeline functional decomposition. However, the domain (here, the image being processed) must also be distributed, and so it is also a domain decomposition.

However, the techniques described earlier have been derived from experience with machines consisting of less than 100 processors. The next generation of machines will likely be composed of thousands of processors. The programmer must determine whether the programming techniques will scale.

One way to deal with the problem is simply to allocate hundreds of processors to tens of programs, but that does not really address the programming question. In fact, some problems have meaningful data sets that will require the larger computational power. This includes problems that, because of existing computational power, are currently solved in two dimensions but could be solved in three dimensions with more power. Examples of this kind of problem include weather simulation, fluid flow, and structural analysis. Other problems, such as complete molecular dynamics calculations, could also be solved using current techniques but would require thousands of processors.

However, not every problem will scale to a sufficient size to require resources of a thousand processors by itself. More often, these applications will be parts of larger applications, solving problems as yet computationally too expensive. In this case, these applications will be modules or components of the overall computation which involves different software technologies such as numerics and artificial intelligence. With parallel programming, the opportunity arises to decompose the software first into modules according to the software technology, and further according to the type of decomposition that best fits the module.

Layered Parallelism Applied to Search Trees

For applications that involve search trees, it may be effective to use more than one search algorithm. When one algorithm finds the answer, the processes running the other algorithms would be stopped. Each algorithm could be run simultaneously on a subset of the nodes. This is a functional decomposition at this level, because each processing resource is performing a different function.

At the next level, for those algorithms that use iteration, you could distribute the iterations over an appropriate number of processors (perfectly parallel decomposition). The data base being searched could also be decomposed (domain decomposition). This, then, produces layered parallelism.

Applying these techniques successfully to an application multiplies the number of processors that can be operating effectively in parallel at each level. For example, five-fold parallelism at the top level, ten-fold parallelism at each of the first sub-levels, and ten-fold parallelism at the second sub-level (for each parent on the first sublevel) produces 500-fold parallelism.

Layered Parallelism in Seismic Monitoring

Another large-scale example that could use layered parallelism is the problem of seismic monitoring.

This kind of application involves a number of very different functions that are best implemented in different languages. This offers the opportunity to decompose the software first into modules according to the software technology, and further according to the type of decomposition that best fits the module.

An example of how this might work is that real-time signals come in from monitors located at various sites such as active volcanos. Each signal is cleaned up by a Fortran program, and given to a C program that runs a neural network that translates the signals to symbols. These signals are then given to an AI program (in Lisp) that interprets them to determine whether an event of interest is occurring at present. This program also stores samples of incoming signals in a database to produce a baseline.

When an event of interest does occur, another AI program is called to interpret the real time data coming in. This AI program needs additional signal processing help, so it uses additional resources. The AI program interpreting the event of interest must make use of the baseline data base.

This whole package must be replicated for each volcano being monitored, because each has a different geology, and so the baseline database for each is different.

Therefore, at the top level, the application is perfectly parallel, in that the same processing is available for the signals coming in from each of the volcanoes being monitored. On the next level, functional parallelism is used to clean up, translate, interpret, and store the signals. Interpretation of real-time data may require domain decomposition for each signal. Figure 6.6 illustrates this decomposition.

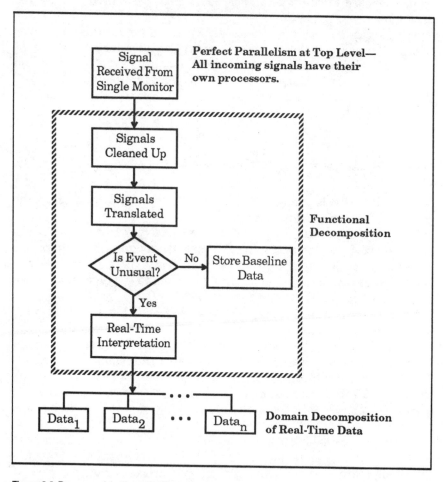

Figure 6.6 Decomposing the seismic monitoring problem.

Summary

Control decomposition is an approach that focuses on distributing the flow of control rather than distributing the domain. It is a method that works well for problems in which the domain is not static and regular.

For very large applications, it may be necessary to use more than one decomposition technique to solve the problem efficiently. This layered approach is likely to be used more in the future for solving complex problems on systems of thousands of processors.

The next chapter introduces another approach to parallel program design: object-oriented decomposition techniques.

7

Object-Oriented Techniques for Distributed-Memory Systems

Previous chapters have introduced domain and control decomposition, two techniques that can help extract parallelism from various applications. Domain decomposition focuses primarily on a program's data structures and control decomposition focuses on the distinct threads of execution.

This chapter introduces object-oriented programming for distributed-memory systems. An object-oriented approach to programming provides a formal basis for organizing the data structures and threads of execution of which a program consists. It is possible with this technique to express these decompositions clearly and in a way that makes it possible to catch errors early in the design cycle.

The next section defines objects, the basis of object-oriented programming, and how an object-oriented approach is used to construct sequential programs. Following that is an exploration of how object-oriented programming can be applied to the design of parallel programs, and, in particular, to the techniques of domain and control decomposition.

Three examples are used to explain this technique. The first solves the matrix factoring problem first presented in Chapter 5 as a domain decomposition example. The second solves the triangle problem, introduced in Chapter 6 as an example of control decomposition. The final example combines both of these techniques and describes an air traffic control simulation.

What Are Objects?

Object-oriented programming was developed originally for sequential systems, to address the problems associated with software complexity. This approach is readily adaptable to the development of large applications for distributed-memory parallel systems. Object-oriented techniques are most helpful when you need to organize and manage large programs. While certain emerging programming languages such as C++ and, to some extent, ADA, support these techniques, you can implement object-oriented techniques in most languages.

In object-oriented programming, the general term for object decomposition is data abstraction. This means that you decompose a program's data structures and procedures into smaller parts (objects) based on the semantics of the entities represented by the data and the semantics of the interactions among those entities. Objects encompass related data and the procedures that understand and manipulate that data, encapsulating both item and function. Figure 7.1 illustrates this.

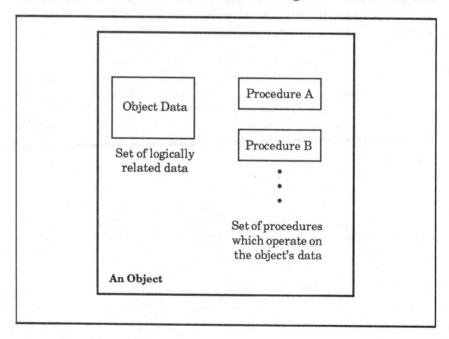

Figure 7.1 An object's structure.

For example, a program may use a stack as temporary storage. In an object-oriented program, you can define the data structures required to implement the stack. You would also specify the set of operations that manage the stack, such as **push** and **pop**. This defines a new data type, the "stack" type, which you can then use in creating program variables, as shown in Figure 7.2.

The definition of an object type (or class) is separate from the creation of instances of the object type, which are simply called objects.

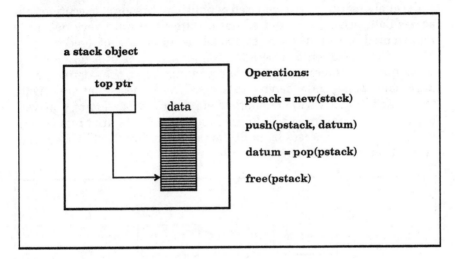

Figure 7.2 Defining the stack as an object.

Only the object's procedures have access to the object's data. A programmer does not need to know how an object is implemented, only how to use the object's procedures. This can simplify the design of large programs because many of the implementation details can be hidden from view.

Data abstraction has other advantages that have impact throughout the design cycle. It simplifies debugging by restricting the number of procedures that you need to examine to determine why a program state was incorrectly altered. It simplifies testing by defining clean interfaces that can be rigorously tested. It allows you to change the implementation of an object freely (e.g., to improve performance) without modifying the rest of the program.

Object Decomposition for Parallel Architectures

Object-oriented techniques provide a bridge from the sequential world to the parallel world. After defining the object types, with their attendant data structures and functions, you have done most of what you need to do to adapt the application to a parallel system.

Parallel programs are very naturally described by object-oriented models, and this formulation provides excellent hints to the system for partitioning data structures across the system's processing nodes.

Parallel programs are composed of multiple threads of execution that access both private and shared data. Data values are very naturally represented within the object model as instances of object types. Threads of execution can be allocated as instances of a task type. If tasks must communicate by exchanging messages, they define procedures for sending and receiving messages. Data objects that are private to a task interact with one another via direct invocation of a private object's functional interface. Shared data structures are organized as objects, with their access by multiple tasks synchronized by a system-defined class of queue objects, as illustrated in Figure 7.3.

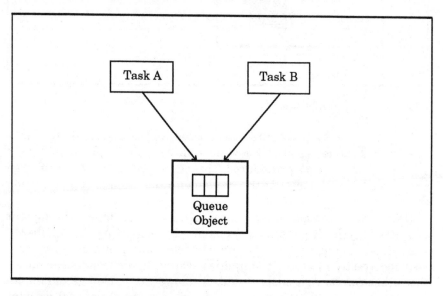

Figure 7.3 Shared access to a queue object by multiple tasks.

Object decomposition offers certain advantages for parallel systems. It inherently avoids the use of global variables, simplifying the job of partitioning data and code across the processing nodes. In addition, the use of procedures to access objects provides a higher granularity of interaction than does direct access to object variables. This can improve the efficiency of the underlying message-passing system.

Programming tools are available for object-oriented programming on parallel machines. As mentioned earlier, the ADA language supports data abstraction, and programming tools such as Interwork II can greatly simplify the programming task, providing global object name space and automatic message-passing and load-balancing facilities. These and other tools are described in the next chapter.

Partial Gaussian Elimination

The first example looks at the partial gaussian elimination used earlier as an example of domain decomposition. Partial gaussian elimination is a technique for factoring a matrix that is used in solving linear equations. A sequential version of the algorithm can be summarized as follows:

```
for (all columns i)
   Select_max (column i);
      for (all columns j>i)
          Transform (column j using column i)
      end for
end for
```

The **Select_max** procedure encapsulates several operations, including selecting the maximum value in column i, swapping this element with the ith element, and normalizing all elements. The **Transform** procedure swaps the same two element positions in the jth column (thus swapping two rows of the matrix in total), and then it transforms the values of column j using values from column i.

This algorithm manipulates the columns of a matrix. A matrix is represented as a one-dimensional array of columns. It is convenient, therefore, to define the object type *column* associated with the procedures **Select_max** and **Transform** to manipulate objects of this type. You would also need other procedures to initialize and print the values within a column. By defining the **Select_max** and **Transform** procedures on *column* objects, you can define precisely how the column data is manipulated by various portions of the algorithm.

You can construct a parallel version of the algorithm as a straight-forward extension of the sequential algorithm:

```
for (all columns i)
    Select_max (column i);
    do in parallel for (all columns j>i)
        Transform (column j using column i)
    end for
end for
```

Notice that the **Transform** procedure is executed in parallel for all columns $j>i$. Just as was done in the earlier domain decomposition example of this problem, you first partition the columns of the matrix across the processing nodes. The **Transform** operation is executed on all of the column objects in parallel. Figure 7.4 illustrates the distribution of the columns across the nodes.

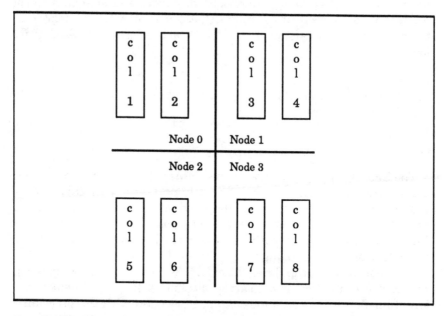

Figure 7.4 Distribution of column objects across the nodes.

To eliminate the need for global synchronization between steps of the inner for-loop, the algorithm can be reorganized by wrapping the **Select** and **Transform** procedures within two new procedures operating on a column object, as follows:

```
Select_and_transform(column i) {
   Select_max(column i);
   do in parallel for (all columns j > i)
     Transform_and_select(column j using column i, pivot)
   end do
}

Transform_and_select(column j using column i, pivot) {
   Transform(column j using column i, pivot);
   if (i < N) {
     Select_and_transform(column i+1)
   }
}
```

Execution is initiated by invoking **Select_and_transform** on column 1 of N columns. Program execution is carried out as a sequence of operations on column objects, most of which are executed in parallel, as illustrated in Figure 7.5.

The sequence of operations for this algorithm is precisely the same as the sequence for the parallel algorithm in Chapter 5. It differs in its explicit definition of column objects and its focus on the "logical" parallelism provided in transforming these objects. The object-oriented style explicitly describes the data structures and the procedures that operate on them — it focuses on logical entities and the behavior and interaction of those entities.

In contrast, the algorithm in Chapter 5 represents columns as simple arrays, which can be manipulated by any code within the program. It also focuses on the parallelism between processors, instead of the parallelism between columns. This causes the algorithm to combine the code that manipulates a column with the code that multiplexes the management of multiple columns on a given node. The object-oriented algorithm, on the other hand, separates out the multiplexing code into the "do parallel" step — the focus is on the implementation strategy itself.

Control Decomposition: The Triangle Problem

The triangle problem used as a control decomposition example in Chapter 6 can also be designed and implemented using an object-oriented approach. The basic algorithm uses three object types:

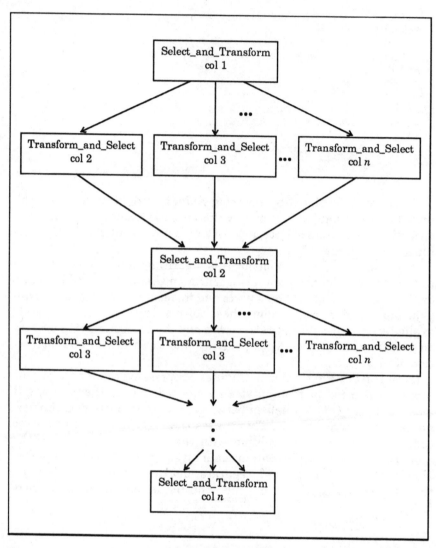

Figure 7.5 Sequence of object invocations in the PGE algorithm.

- *configuration* object
  Instances of this type describe a configuration of the triangle playboard between moves.

- *move* object
  Describes a move on the playboard.

- *move sequence* object
  Describes a sequence of moves (i.e., *move* objects) made during the game.

  Move sequence objects have three principal operations:

- **store_move** (*move sequence, move*)
  This adds a move to the sequence.

- **remove_move** (*move sequence*)
  This deletes the last move from the sequence.

- **store_solution** (*move sequence*)
  This records the move sequence as a solution to the problem.

  Objects of type *configuration* have four principal operations:

- *move* = **Generate_next_move** (*configuration, previous move*)
  This generates the next move in a search of moves based on a previous unsuccessful move from this configuration.

- **Undo_last_move** (*configuration*)
  This undoes the previous move and restores the previous playboard configuration.

- *depth* = **Get_search_depth** (*configuration*)
  This returns the search depth that led to the current configuration.

- *move sequence* = **Get_move_sequence** (*configuration*)
  This returns the sequence of moves that led to the current configuration

  Note that **Generate_next_move** returns an instance of a move object, which describes the move that was made. It also updates the *configuration* object to reflect the move. This object type encapsulates the search depth as part of the definition of a configuration. **Generate_next_move** increments the search depth, and **Undo_last_move** decrements it. The type also encapsulates a move sequence object that describes how the configuration was generated from the initial configuration (each *configuration* object has its own private *move sequence* object). This sequence is retrieved with **Get_move_sequence**.

These object definitions allow the sequential triangle algorithm (shown in Chapter 6) to be rewritten as follows:

```
configuration = Create_object (configuration type)
call Depth_first_search (configuration)

Depth_first_search (configuration) {
  if Get_search_depth (configuration) = 14 {
    Store _solution (Get_move_sequence (configuration))
  } else {
    move = Generate_next_move (configuration)
    while move is not NULL {
      call Depth_first_search (configuration, move)
      Undo_last_move (configuration)
      move = Generate_next_move (configuration)
    }
  }
  return
}
```

Notice that this object-oriented formulation formalizes the data structures used in the program and the operations that affect them. The object-oriented approach also clarifies the data that must be transmitted between the manager and the workers in a parallel version of this algorithm. In particular, the manager must send each worker a configuration.

The worker then explores the configuration for solutions by calling **Depth_first_search**, returning solutions as they are found. All solutions take the form of a *move sequence* object, which is returned to the manager.

The parallel algorithm must include communication between the manager and the worker processes. As seen earlier, the processes themselves can be treated as objects, with the operations defined on them for sending and receiving objects. Alternatively, the manager's work queue can be treated as an object into which the manager deposits configuration objects, and from which the workers retrieve them. Solutions are returned in another queue object that holds move sequences. (The underlying object programming system would need to be able to locate this work queue on a remote node for worker processes distributed across the system.) This approach is illustrated in Figure 7.6.

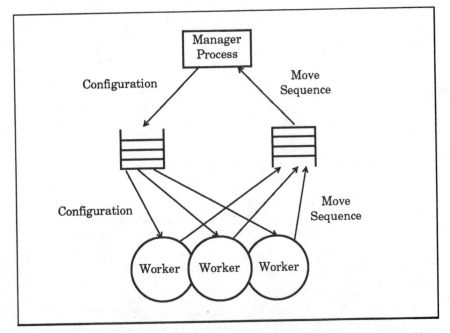

Figure 7.6 Object oriented formulation of manager/worker decomposition in the triangle problem.

There are three procedures defined for the *queue* object type needed for the work and solution queues:

- **Enqueue** (*queue, object*), which enqueues an object into the queue.
- *object* = **Dequeue** (*queue*), which removes an object from the queue.
- **Terminate_enqueuing** (*queue*), which indicates that no more items will be enqueued (by a NULL return to Dequeue) once all sources have executed this procedure.

Using this new object type, the **Depth_first_search** procedure can be modified to generate several partial solutions and enqueue them into the work queue. The manager's code uses this to create work items for its worker tasks. The queue object also maintains information required to signal its users that no more items will be enqueued. This is needed to synchronize the manager and workers when the program is complete.

The manager task creates the queues and worker tasks. It then enqueues several partial solutions and awaits solutions from the workers:

```
work_queue = Create_object (queue type, 1 source)
solution_queue = Create_object (queue type, NUM_WORKERS sources)
repeat NUM_WORKERS times {
   Create_object (task type, work_queue, solution_queue)
}
configuration = Create_object (configuration type)
Create_partial_solutions (configuration)
Terminate_enqueuing (work_queue)
configuration = Dequeue (solution_queue)
while configuration is not NULL {
   Store_solution (configuration)
      configuration = Dequeue(solution_queue)
}


Create_partial_solutions (configuration) {
   if Get_search_depth (configuration) = threshold {
     Enqueue (work_queue, Get_move_sequence (configuration))
   }
   else {
     move = Generate_next_move (configuration)
     while move is not NULL {
        call Depth_first_search (configuration, move)
        Undo_last_move (configuration)
        move = Generate_next_move (configuration)
     }
   }
   return
}
```

The worker's code repeatedly removes work from the work queue and
enqueues solutions into the solution queue:

```
configuration = Dequeue (work_queue)
while configuration is not NULL {
   call Depth_first_search (configuration)
   configuration = Dequeue (work_queue)
}
Terminate_enqueuing (solution_queue)

Depth_first_search (configuration) {
   if Get_search_depth (configuration) = 14 {
      Enqueue(solution_queue, Get_move_sequence (configuration))
   }
   else {
   move = Generate_next_move (configuration)
   while move is not NULL
{    call Depth_first_search (configuration, move)
      Undo_last_move (configuration)
      move = Generate_next_move (configuration)
      }
   }
   return
}
```

Air Traffic Simulation

Object-oriented programming can be very useful in constructing large discrete event simulations. Their naturally modular data structures fit the object-oriented programming model well.

An interesting example of a large discrete event simulation is the model of air traffic flow within the U.S. The goal of this simulation is to measure the effects of scheduling, weather, etc. on the flow of air traffic. Parallel MIMD systems with large memory capacity (such as the iPSC system) allow large simulation models such as this to be held entirely in primary memory; this avoids the delays encountered in paging simulation data to and from backing store.

This parallel discrete event simulation illustrates the use of both domain and control decomposition techniques in an object-oriented formulation.

This model contains three fundamental object types:

- *airports*, which contain information regarding their location and runways
- *airplanes*, which have position, velocity, fuel capacity, etc.
- *air space sectors*

Objects of these types are manipulated by three task types:

- *airline dispatchers*, which schedule (i.e., allocate) airplanes and pilots.
- *pilots*, which operate airplanes
- *air traffic controllers*, which manage the use of airports and airspace sectors by sequencing departures and arrivals.

These object types are illustrated in Figure 7.7.

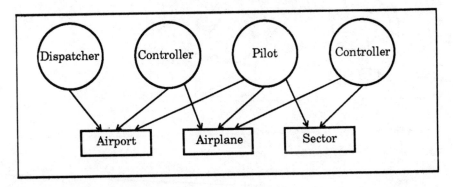

Figure 7.7 Air traffic simulation objects.

The tasks interact by invoking procedures on shared airplane and airport objects. For example, a pilot requests departure clearance at the airport that is the current location of the airplane. The corresponding controller dequeues requests and sends clearances to the corresponding airplanes. The pilots await the arrival of clearances at their airplanes. They instruct their airplanes to move according to their flight plans toward the destination airports, where this protocol is repeated. The use of multiple tasks with separate functions in this application is an example of control decomposition on a functional basis.

One of the goals of the air traffic simulation is to predict and avoid possible collisions between aircraft during their flights. To control the computational complexity of this problem, the airspace is partitioned into sectors, and an air traffic controller manages the separation of aircraft within each sector. The sectors and their controllers are illustrated in Figure 7.8.

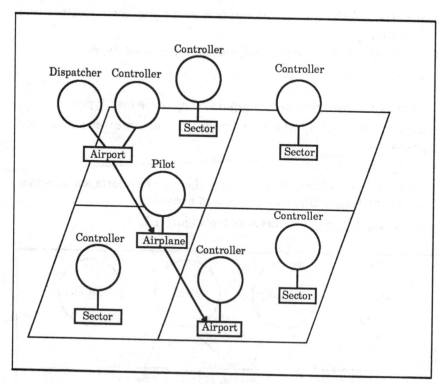

Figure 7.8 Modeling the airspace.

In the object-oriented formulation, each airspace sector is represented as an object of type sector. Sector objects maintain a list of aircraft flying across their portion of the airspace. An air traffic controller task is assigned to each sector; this task examines the list for possible collisions and redirects aircraft as necessary.

The sector objects (a domain decomposition of the problem) form an excellent basis for distributing the simulation across the nodes of the parallel system. This domain decomposition of the airspace allows the controller tasks to execute in parallel in different sectors. It also allows the distribution of airports across the processing nodes by associating the airports and their associated controller tasks with the airspace sectors in which they reside. As airplanes "fly" from one airport to another, the objects are sent from node to node as they move through the airspace sectors.

The load balance achieved with this partitioning depends upon how evenly airplanes and airports are distributed throughout the airspace. You can use various techniques to improve the load balance:

• The sector boundaries could reflect expected traffic densities.

• The sector objects can be interleaved across the processing nodes instead of being distributed conformally.

• Sectors can migrate dynamically between nodes as the air traffic density changes.

Summary

Object-oriented programming techniques can be effectively applied to the design of concurrent programs. These techniques can simplify the programmer's view of large programs. They also provide a basis for distributing these programs across the system's processing nodes and for efficiently accessing these data.

8

Parallel Programming Tools: Developing a Better Mousetrap

With the proliferation of varied architectures offering reliable, high-speed computation, the evolution of software tools for parallel computing is starting to accelerate. A set of emerging tools is making the job of the programmer easier, and work is under way on more advanced tools.

These tools are evolutionary rather than revolutionary, and focus on simplifying the programming process and optimizing the code. Some are built on existing languages, while others rely on the development of new languages. In many cases, you can use existing code while still moving ahead with these tools.

Figure 8.1 shows the evolution of the complete tool set.

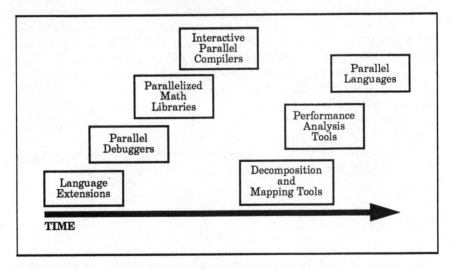

Figure 8.1 The evolution of the parallel programing tool set.

Program development tools to fill most of these blocks have already started to appear, with more being developed all the time. Development has followed the programmer's most immediate needs. First, you need to be able to express a program, with libraries of routines that add parallel function, extended languages, or a combination of both. Debuggers are then required to make the program work. Finally, you need tools to help you optimize your program: math libraries, performance analysis tools, etc. Tools designed to aid algorithm design and true parallel languages are being developed, but that development has lagged the development of coding tools.

Parallel Debugging Tools

The complexity of parallel systems makes having a good debugger, designed for the parallel programming model, a requirement. You need to have a clear view of what is occurring on all nodes used in the execution of a program. It is also important to be able to trace messages, because many of the errors in parallel programs tend to be in interprocessor communication.

One such debugger is the iPSC Interactive Parallel Debugger. It provides the features expected of a symbolic source-level debugger for serial programs, including full execution control with breakpoints, single stepping, display of source code, and disassembly. To implement parallel debugging, you can specify debug contexts — groups of nodes on which you want to control execution or view results. Whenever you are looking at more than one node, it displays information on all of those. You can also see the message queues to see, at any given time, messages that have been sent but not received, or are expected but not yet received.

Sophisticated parallel debuggers such as this one are starting to reduce the time required to write parallel code.

Math Libraries and Solvers

Most of the applications required of parallel computers are computationally intensive. Mathematics tools are available for parallel systems so the programmer need not re-invent them. Serial mathematics libraries such as BLAS (Basic Linear Algebra Subprograms) and NAG (Numerical Algorithms Group) have been ported to most parallel systems, to provide sophisticated mathematical functions. BLAS consists of three sets of routines: BLAS I, providing vector-vector operations, BLAS II, for vector-matrix operations, and BLAS III, for matrix-matrix operations. NAG offers routines for advanced matrix operations (based on BLAS routines), eigenvalues and eigenvectors, differentiation, integration, solution of partial differentials, complex arithmetic, simple calculation on statistical data, correlation and regression analysis, and more. Use of these libraries requires that the programmer assign the routines to the nodes.

More advance parallel mathematics tools, such as matrix solvers, are becoming available. Matrices are classified as either sparse or dense, and solvers implement their solution using either iterative or direct methods. Further, the size of the matrix to be solved dictates the way the solver works. Some solvers require that all data be memory resident (in-core) while others are designed to store the complete data set in mass storage and swap in sections of the matrix at a time for solution.

An example of a matrix solver tool set is the iPSC ProSolver series. ProSolver-SES is a direct, in-core solver for sparse matrices; ProSolver-IES is an iterative, in-core solver for sparse matrices, and Pro-Solver-DES is a direct, out-of-core solver for dense matrices.

All of these tools make it easier to create complex, computationally intensive applications.

Parallel Program Development Tools

An array of new tools have already emerged to aid parallel program development, and more are being developed all the time. These include interactive parallel compilers and tools to aid decomposition and mapping. Table 8.1 lists a few.

An Interactive Parallelizing System

CAST, from Pacific-Sierra Research, is a powerful set of interactive tools for parallel programming. These tools significantly simplify the

TABLE 8.1   Some Emerging Parallel Programming Tools

CAST	An interactive parallelizing system
Interwork II	An object-oriented programming tool kit
Strand	An integration tool and parallel language
Linda	An associative memory programming tool
SVM	A shared memory operating system

task of creating efficient parallel programs in Fortran. With these tools, you can either convert existing sequential Fortran programs into efficient parallel programs, or you can design and implement new parallel algorithms. Where automatic parallelizing compilers can only extract the low-level parallelism that may exist in sequential code, CAST helps restructure code at a higher level to produce more efficient algorithms. The development of true parallelizing compilers for MIMD machines is an area of active research, but for now it is up to the programmer to determine the decomposition.

Where the task is to convert existing sequential code, CAST provides comprehensive analytical information about the sequential code, including interprocedural data dependencies. With restructuring tools and graphic representation of the data flow, you can manipulate code blocks to create more efficient structures. Analytic data about the new structures ensures the integrity and stability of the application. A code generator then produces Fortran source code for execution on the desired target machine. The generated code may be instrumented to help you gauge the effectiveness of the algorithm and allow for iterative optimization of the code.

An Object-Oriented Programming Tool Kit

The Interwork II Concurrent Programming Toolkit, from Block Island Technologies, is an object-oriented tool kit that allows programmers to take advantage of the object-oriented programming model (introduced in Chapter 7), while considerably simplifying the programming task. It provides facilities for writing parallel programs within the C language. It is designed to support an object-oriented programming model independent of the underlying parallel architecture, while allowing the programmer to reap the system's high performance.

At the foundation of Interwork II's programming model is a global object name space that spans the memories of all processing nodes. This facility allows programmers to create objects and then directly invoke their procedures from remote nodes; its semantics closely match the object-oriented model of the C++ language. The global name space simplifies the programmer's job by eliminating the need to locate remote objects and send messages to invoke their procedures. Objects can be dynamically created and destroyed during a program's execution. They can also transparently migrate between processing nodes as they are accessed by processes.

Interwork II supports a "lightweight" process model, in which all processes within one node reside in the same shared address space. The reduced complexity of these processes allows the programmer to create hundreds or thousands of processes per node (depending only on the available memory), and it ensures very fast context switching between them. Interwork II processes are treated as globally named objects, which allows them to be uniformly accessed throughout the system.

To simplify the construction of large, parallel programs, Interwork II enables the programmer to create multi-dimensional arrays of objects. Interwork II automatically partitions these objects across the processing nodes. Object procedures can be broadcast to all element objects, and data can be combined from the elements. These arrays are typically used to implement domain decompositions (such as the air traffic simulation in Chapter 7). They allow the domain decomposition to be viewed logically by the programmer and then automatically mapped to the underlying parallel architecture.

Although Interwork II currently supports only arrays of objects, it provides the tools needed by the programmer to create other types of *aggregate* objects, that is, collections of logically related objects, such as distributed B-trees or associatively accessed tuples. The programmer defines an access mechanism for the object collection (analogous to the index mechanism used for arrays) and specifies how the objects are to be mapped to the parallel architecture.

Discrete event simulations require a global time base to synchronize the actions of the processes. Interwork II provides a time base that spans the processing nodes. This allows processes in different nodes to share a common time base, thus making the underlying architecture transparent to the programmer.

Low level communication between nodes in accomplished using a remote procedure call mechanism in Interwork II. This simplifies the invocation of procedures on remote nodes, and it eliminates the need to explicitly send and receive messages.

Interwork II's tools are organized as a C language program library, to which the application links prior to execution. Once the program is loaded into all nodes of the system, execution begins in one initial process. This process creates the appropriate objects and processes needed to represent the application's data structures and threads of execution.

Interwork II has been used primarily in parallel discrete event simulations, such as the simulation of large parallel computer architectures and air traffic control simulation. It is currently being applied to a broader range of applications, including numerical applications and manager/worker problems.

A General Purpose Parallel Programming Language

Another approach to parallel programming is called Strand, a general-purpose high-level symbolic parallel programming language from Artificial Intelligence Limited for all classes of parallel computers. The language was developed to have the best features to come from the development of Flat Concurrent Prolog and Parlog. One of the benefits of the approach taken is that it is possible to move programs in Strand between very different architectures with little or no modification.

The language uses logic variables to handle communication and synchronization. The binding environment for variables is implicitly distributed among the processors with fast inter-processor reading or assignment of variables. As a result, the programmer does not need to add parallelism explicitly. The program may be distributed among the processors by direct allocation or some system-supplied mapping.

Strand also offers a high-level parallel integration tool that allows you to use existing modules, providing programming "glue" to join them into a parallel program. If the modules are in different languages, it offers an inter-language interface. It simplifies communication and synchronization by use of logic variables.

An Associative Memory Programming Tool

One of the difficulties of programming a distributed-memory parallel system is the need to know where information is and to send and receive needed information explicitly from one node to another. The Linda associative memory tool takes over this job from the programmer.

Linda uses the model of "tuple" space. A tuple is a piece of information that may either be code or data. (The name "tuple" is derived by generalizing numerical words for multiple, like quintuple.) Linda coordinates program design by remembering the last location of tuples to make them available whenever they are needed, without requiring the programmer to be concerned about communication paths and synchronization.

Linda uses simple constructs to extend existing languages, so that you can build a parallel program from smaller programs that may be in more than one language.

A Shared Memory Operating System

The problem of making parallel programming easier has also been attacked at the operating system and library level.

Currently available for distributed memory machines is a shared-memory operating system, SVM (Shared Virtual Memory). This portable platform provides a global shared linear address space for all processes. It uses a read-mostly memory model as its data structure. It assigns memory blocks on different nodes physical pages (implemented with page protection bits) to maintain coherency of memory.

Performance Analysis Tools

An array of performance analysis tools is now on the market from various vendors, and more are being developed and refined all the time. As has been stressed throughout this book, tuning your program is a required part of parallel program development. A performance analyzer can considerably reduce your time and effort in this area. It can help you see the strength and weaknesses of a particular parallelization scheme, and once you are satisfied that the general algorithm design is appropriate, it can help you determine quickly where in the program you need to spend most of your time and effort to improve the performance of areas within your program.

One such is the Parallel Performance Analysis Tool (PAT) from Parasoft Corporation. Using a graphical interface, it provides an execution profiler that monitors the time spent in individual routines, a communication profiler that assesses time spent in communication and I/O, and an event profiler that shows the interactions between processors and allows you to monitor events of specific interest.

Future Steps

The next steps in the development of parallel software tools will be the development of parallelizing compilers, and further advances in the development of program development tools. Early versions of parallel languages are available, such as C* and Fortran D for SIMD systems. Development of parallel programming tools is proceeding at such a rapid pace, however, that any list of tools is likely to be out of date by the time it is printed.

In general, while a collection of tools is currently available, the movement is toward creating a cohesive tool set. In the future, a shared graphic interface is likely to be developed that will allow this tool set to be ported across different parallel architectures, making the tools, and therefore the capabilities of the systems, more widely available.

Code Examples

This appendix contains examples of coded implementations of some of the algorithms described in this book. All examples were implemented on the iPSC system.

There are four examples:

- The calculation of pi (also listed in Chapter 3 of this book)
- Sections of the seismic simulation code
- Implementation of the two-dimensional FFT routine
- Implementation of the triangle problem

For more information on parallel programming routines for the iPSC systems, contact Intel Supercomputer Systems Division.

The Pi Calculation

The following Fortran code is an implementation of the simple pi calculation listed in Chapter 3 of this book for the iPSC systems.

```
f(x) = 4.0/(1.0 + x*x)
integer n, i, p, me, mpid
real w, x, sum, pi

p = numnodes()                                    return the number of nodes
me = mynode()                                     return my node's number
mpid = mypid()                                    return my process id
msglen = 4                                        define length of message
allnds = -1                                       define term for all nodes
msgtp0 = 0                                         define term for message type 0
msgtp1 = 1                                         define term for message type 1

if (me .eq. 0) then                               if I am node 0,
  read *, n                                        read the number of strips
  call csend(msgtp0, n, msglen, allnds, mpid)     and send it to all nodes
else                                              If I am any other node
  call crecv(msgtp0, n, msglen)                   receive the value of n
endif

w = 1.0/n

sum = 0.0

do 10 i = me+1, n, p                              deal out the strips to the processors
  x = w*(i-0.5)
  sum = sum + f(x)
10 continue

call gssum(sum, 1, temp)                          call global summing operation
if (me .eq. 0) then                               if I am node 0
  pi = w*sum                                       calculate final value
  print *, pi                                      and print
endif
```

Seismic Simulation Code

The seismic simulation algorithm was implemented on the iPSC-VX vector system, in Fortran with calls to the vector library routines. To obtain the best performance of the iPSC/2-VX computer, the wave equation interior computation (*) was implemented in special-purpose microcode for the vector processor, after first coding it as a Fortran double loop and then as a single loop of vector operations. The Fortran code implementing (*) for each interior point of a strip belonging to one processor, uses nine floating-point operations per gridpoint.

```
      do 20 j = 2,irgt-1
        do 10 i = 2,imax-1
        u(i,j,kv) = 2.*u(i,j,ku) - u(i,j,kv)
    +      +    csq(i,j) * ( u(i+1,j,ku) + u(i-1,j,ku)
    +      +    u(i,j+1,ku) + u(i,j-1,ku) - 4.*u(i,j,ku) )
10    continue
20    continue
```

This computation can be expressed as a sequence of vector operations acting on the columns of the strip, using the native vector library routines available for the vector processor.

```
      do 10 j = 2,irgt-1
c           v = -v -- 0 ops
      call sneg (imax-2, u(2,j,kv), 1)

c           v = 2*u + v
      call saxpy (imax-2, 2., u(2,j,ku), 1, u(2,j,kv), 1)

c           temp = u + u -- 1 op
        call svadd (imax-2, u(2,j-1,ku), 1, u(2,j+1,ku), 1, temp, 1)

c           temp = u + temp -- 1 op
      call svadd (imax-2, u(1,j,ku), 1, temp, 1, temp, 1)

c           temp = u + temp -- 1 op
      call svadd (imax-2, u(3,j,ku), 1, temp, 1, temp, 1)

c        temp = -4*u + temp -- 2 ops
      call saxpy (imax-2, -4., u(2,j,ku), 1, temp, 1)

c        temp = csq*temp -- 1 op
      call svmul (imax-2, csq(2,j), 1, temp, 1, temp, 1)

c        v = v + temp -- 1 op
      call svadd (imax-2, u(2,j,kv), 1, temp, 1, u(2,j,kv), 1)

c        Total 9 ops
10    continue
```

You can implement vector operations efficiently on the i860 microprocessor using the **pfld** command to access two 32-bit quantities every second cycle. Storing results takes three cycles for each 64-bit quantity. Thus, each of the vector operations will bememory baound and not approach the peak performance of the chip. The best rate obtainable from the vector approach is about 20 MFLOPS. To approach peak performance, you need to write an i860 assembly language routine that implements the entire kernel at once. With careful use of the cache, you can obtain a rate of almost 50 MFLOPS.

The following code maps the strips to the nodes using natural ordering.

```
c    Map strips to nodes using the natural ordering.
        if (mynode().eq.0) then
           mypred = -1
        else
           mypred = mod (mynode()+numnodes()-1, nproc)
        endif
        if (mynode().eq.nproc-1) then
           mysucc = -1
        else
           mysucc = mod (mynode()+1, nproc)
        endif

c    Call assembly code for interior of strip.
        call sfive (u(1,3,ku), u(1,3,kv), c(1,3), imax, irgt-4)

c    Set up to receive messages, then send messages out.
        if (mypred.ne.-1)
     +      ipred = irecv (nsucc, u(1,1,ku), 4*imax)
        if (mysucc.ne.-1)
     +      isucc = irecv (npred, u(1,irgt,ku), 4*imax)
        if (mypred.ne.-1)
     +       call csend (npred, u(1,2,ku),4*imax,mypred,mypid())
        if (mysucc.ne.-1)
     + call csend (nsucc, u(1,irgt-1,ku),4*imax,mysucc,mypid())

c    Wait for the messages to arrive.
        if (mypred.ne.-1) call msgwait (ipred)
        if (mysucc.ne.-1) call msgwait (isucc)

c    Call assembly code for left edge of strip.
        call sfive (u(1,2,ku), u(1,2,kv), c(1,2), imax, 1)
```

```
c      Call assembly code for right edge of strip.
       call sfive (u(1,irgt-1,ku), u(1,irgt-1,kv),
     +          c(1,irgt-1), imax, 1)
```

2D-FFT Code

The two-dimensional FFT (Fast Fourier Transform) routine talked about in Chapter 5 of this book was implemented in Fortran for the iPSC system.

```
subroutine fft2d(m, a, p, buf,b)
integer m, p
complex a(m,*), t, buf(*), b(*)
include 'fcube.h'
c
integer xor
integer node, pid
integer me, pid, node
integer n, i, it, nstart
integer csize
parameter (csize = 8)

me = mynode()
pid = mypid()

if(me .ge. p) return
n = m*p

do 20 i = 1, m
call cfft(n, a(i,1), m, b, 1)
call dcopy(n, b, 1, a(i,1), m)
20 continue

c
do 30 i = 1,p-1
node = xor(me,i)
it = irecv(i, buf, csize*m*m)
call csend(i, a(1,m*node +1), csize*m*m, node, pid)
call msgwait(it)
call ctrans(me, me, buf, a(1,m*node+1))
30 continue
c
```

```
c local transpose
c
call dcopy(me*me, a(1,m*me+1), 1, buf, 1)
call ctrans(me, me, buf, a(1,m*me+1))


do 40 i = 1, m
call cfft(n, a(i,1), m, b, 1)
call dcopy(n, b, 1, a(i,1), m)
40 continue

return
end
subroutine ctrans(n, m, a, b)
integer n, m
complex a(n,m), b(m,n)
c
c this subroutine transposes a into b
c
include 'fcube.h'
integer i

if(n .gt. m) then
do 10 i = 1, m
call dcopy(n, a(1,i), 1, b(i,1), m)
10 continue
else
do 20 i = 1, n call dcopy(m, a(i,1), n, b(1,i), 1)
20 continue
endif
return
end
```

The Triangle Problem

This implementation of the triangle algorithm described in Chapter 6
is in the C language. It consists of a host program that loads the manager and worker program onto the cube, a manager program that
explores the tree to a depth of thresh (determined by an argument on
the command line; default is 5). Trees below the depth of thresh are
passed off to a worker.

The Host Program

This program loads the manager and worker programs onto the cube.

```
* manager explores the tree to a depth of thresh, which is
* determined by an argument in the command line. (default is 5).
* Trees below depth of thresh are passed off to a worker.
*
* tri [-hn][-td]
*      where n is the number of the initial empty postion.
*      where d is the threshhold depth.
*
* triangle game:
*                        1
*
*                     2   3
*
*                   4   5   6
*
*                 7   8   9   10
*
*              11  12  13  14   15
*
*/

#include <stdio.h>
#include <cube.h>
#include "trian.h"


char mgr[] = "mgr";
char worker[] = "worker";

void main(argc, argv)
   int argc;
   char *argv[];
{
   int i;
   int hole= 5;                        /* initial missing peg postion */
   int thresh= 4;                        /* mgr dispense threshold */
   int ignore;
   int node_count;
   int result;
   struct start_msgstart;
```

```
setpid(PID);
node_count = numnodes();
if (node_count < 2)
  error("This model requires at least two nodes on the cube.");


/* argument hell */

for (i=1; i<argc; ++i)
{
  if (argv[i][0] == '-')
  {
    switch (argv[i][1])
    {
      case 'h':
        if (argv[i][2] == '\0' && argc >= i)
          {
            hole = atoi(argv[i+1]);
            ++i;
          }
        else
          hole = atoi(argv[i]+2);
        break;

      case 't':
        if (argv[i][2] == '\0' && argc > i)
          {
            thresh = atoi(argv[i+1]);
            ++i;
          }
        else
          thresh = atoi(argv[i]+2);
        break;

      default:
        error("Unknown switch");
    }
  }
  else
    error("tri: usage tri [-tn][-td]");
}
if (thresh<1 || thresh>13)
  error("threshold out of range.");
if (hole<1 || hole>15)
  error("hole out of range.");

/* end of argument hell */
```

```
/* load and start manager process on node 0 */
load(mgr, MGR_NODE, PID);

/* send start parameters to manager. */
start.hole = hole;
start.thresh = thresh;
ignore = isend(START, &start, sizeof(struct start_msg), MGR_NODE,
PID);

/* load worker processes on the other nodes. */
for (i=1; i<node_count; ++i)
  load(worker, i, PID);

/* wait for result and print to screen */
crecv(RESULT, &result, sizeof(result));
printf("found %d solutions.\n", result);
}
```

The Manager Program - The Triangle Problem

The manager explores the tree to a depth of *thresh*, the value of which is passed to it through the command line of the host program. It then passes trees of a depth greater than that off to the workers as they become available.

```
#include <stdio.h>
#include <cube.h>
#include "trian.h"
#include "moves.h"

intnext_worker(void);
voidsend_path(int);
voiddepth_first_search(int);


intsltn_cnt;/* count of solutions found */
intignore;
intthresh;
inthole;



main()
{
  int i;
  int n_workers;/* number of workers */
  int depth = 1;
  int scratch;
```

```
      struct start_msgstart;

      n_workers = numnodes () - 1;
      crecv(START, &start, sizeof(struct start_msg));
      hole = start.hole;
      thresh = start.thresh;

      /* remove first peg (middle by default). */
      board[hole] = 0;

      /* search */
      depth_first_search(depth);

      /* stop workers and collect sum */
      for (i=1; i<=n_workers; ++i)
        ignore = isend(STOP, &generic, sizeof(generic), i, PID);
      gisum(&sltn_cnt, 1, &scratch);

      /* send back count of total solutions found */
      ignore = isend(RESULT, &sltn_cnt, sizeof(sltn_cnt), myhost (), PID);
}


void depth_first_search(int depth)
   /* int depth; depth is the number of empty holes. */
   /* uses globals: board, poss_moves, and sequence */
{
   int i;

   if (depth == 14)
   /* found a solution! */
     ++sltn_cnt;


   else if (depth >= thresh)
   {
   send_path(depth);
   }

   else
   {
     for (i=0; i<NUM_MOVES; ++i)
     {
       if ( (board[ poss_moves[i].from ] == 1)
          &&(board[ poss_moves[i].over ] == 1)
          &&(board[ poss_moves[i].to ]   == 0) )
       {
         /* make the move */
         board[ poss_moves[i].from ] = 0;
         board[ poss_moves[i].over ] = 0;
         board[ poss_moves[i].to ]   = 1;
```

```
        /* save this move in the current sequence */
        sequence[ depth-1 ] = i;

        /* explore the subtree */
        depth_first_search(depth+1);

        /* undo the move */
        board[ poss_moves[i].from ] = 1;
        board[ poss_moves[i].over ] = 1;
        board[ poss_moves[i].to ]   = 0;
      }
    }
  }
}


void send_path(int depth)
{
  int   i;
  int   w;
  struct path_msgmess;

  /* build path message */
  mess.depth = depth;
  for (i = 0; i<depth; ++i)
  {
    mess.sequence[i] = sequence[i];
  }
  mess.hole = hole;
  csend(PATH, &mess, sizeof(struct path_msg), next_worker(), PID);
    ;
}

int next_worker(void)
{
  crecv(READY, &generic, sizeof(generic));
  return (infonode());
}
```

The Worker Program - The Triangle Problem

This program is loaded onto all nodes except the manager node, and causes the node to request a search tree when it is idle, receive the data from the manager node, and return results to the manager.

```
#include <stdio.h>
#include <cube.h>
#include "trian.h"
#include "moves.h"
```

```
void ready(void);
void play(int *);
void depth_first_search(int);
void report(void);
void error(char *);

intme;
intsltn_cnt;
charerr[100];

main()
{
  intdepth;
  intmsg_type;

  me = mynode();

  ready();

  /* get message */
  for(;;)
  {
    while (iprobe(-1) == NO_MSG)
      ;
    msg_type = infotype();
    switch (msg_type)
    {
      case PATH:
        play(&depth);
        depth_first_search(depth);
        ready();
        break;

      case STOP:
        report();
        exit(0);

      defualt:
        sprintf(err, "worker node %d: Unknown message type.", me );
        error(err);
    }
  }
}


void play(int *dp)
  /* int*dp; */
{
  int i;
  int ii;
  struct path_msg mess;
```

```
/* reinitialize board */
for (i=0; i<16; ++i)
  board[i] = 1;

'* play out sequence received in message from manager. */
_ ecv(PATH, &mess, sizeof(struct path_msg));
board[mess.hole] = 0;
*dp = mess.depth;

for (i=0; i < *dp-1; ++i)
{
  int m;

  m = sequence[i] = mess.sequence[i];

  if (board[ poss_moves[m].from ]!=1
   || board[ poss_moves[m].over ]!=1
   || board[ poss_moves[m].to ]!=0)
  {
    sprintf(err, "node %d: Bad move sequence in path
message.\nmove[%d]: %d", me, i, m);
    error(err);
  }
  else
  {
    board[ poss_moves[m].from ]= 0;
    board[ poss_moves[m].over ]= 0;
    board[ poss_moves[m].to ]= 1;
  }
}
}
void depth_first_search(int depth)
  /* int depth; depth is the number of empty holes. */
  /* uses globals: board, pos_moves, and sequence */
{
  int i;


  if (depth == 14)
  /* found a solution! */
    ++sltn_cnt;


  else
  {
    for (i=0; i<NUM_MOVES; ++i)
    {
      if ( (board[ poss_moves[i].from ] == 1)
          && (board[ poss_moves[i].over ] == 1)
          && (board[ poss_moves[i].to ]   == 0) )
      {
        /* make the move */
        board[ poss_moves[i].from ] = 0;
```

```
            board[ poss_moves[i].over ] = 0;
            board[ poss_moves[i].to ]   = 1;

            /* save this move in the current sequence */
            sequence[ depth-1 ] = i;

            /* explore the subtree */
            depth_first_search(depth+1);

            /* undo the move */
            board[ poss_moves[i].from ] = 1;
            board[ poss_moves[i].over ] = 1;
            board[ poss_moves[i].to ]   = 0;
        }
      }
  }
}

void report()
{
  int scratch;

  gisum(&sltn_cnt, 1, &scratch);
}

void ready()
{
  isend(READY, &generic, sizeof(generic), MGR_NODE, PID);
}
```

Glossary

Control decomposition A method of decomposition that focuses on distributing the flow of control rather than the domain. Two control decomposition methods are functional decomposition, and the manager/worker method.

Decomposition The process of breaking down an application into separate processes for execution on different processors. The two main decomposition methods are domain decomposition and control decomposition.

Distributed memory In parallel computers, an architecture in which each processor has its own memory, not accessible directly by other processors. Communication between nodes is usually accomplished by message passing.

Domain decomposition An approach to decomposition that relies on regularity in the data structures of the application, and focuses on distribution of the domain.

Efficiency A measure of performance on parallel systems defined as speed-up per node (see speed-up).

Functional decomposition A method of control decomposition that separates the application into functions. The simplest kind of functional decomposition is pipelining, for an essentially serial operation that must be performed many times. A node or set of nodes is assigned to each step in a process, and tasks are put through the pipeline one after another. This allows most of the processors to be busy most of the time.

Layered decomposition A decomposition scheme for very large complex applications that combines control decomposition and domain decomposition, using different techniques for different levels of the application.

Loosely-coupled A loosely-coupled parallel system consists of a set of processors, each of which has its own memory and processes information independently from other processors. Processors communicate and synchronize their activities by sending and receiving messages. Interaction among processors is low.

Mapping The process of assigning the parts of an application to nodes.

Manager/Worker A type of control decomposition that uses one (or more) nodes to assign tasks to nodes dynamically, as nodes become available during the course of executing an application.

Message The form in which information is passed from one node to another in a distributed-memory parallel computer.

MIMD Multiple Instruction stream, Multiple Data stream. This acronym parallel systems in which each processor has a separate instruction stream. This book describes programming techniques for this type of system.

Node A processing unit in a distributed-memory parallel system. Each node consists of a main processor, memory, and interface to the network. Some nodes also have numeric coprocessors. Each node typically has the computing power of a stand-alone workstation.

Object-oriented programming A programming technique that can be applied to parallel systems. See Chapter 7.

Perfectly parallel Applications that can be run on different nodes with no communication between nodes. Running different cases of the same program simultaneously is the most clear example of perfect parallelism. Applications with little communication only approach perfect parallelism.

Process In a loosely-coupled parallel system, a sequential part of a complete parallel application that runs on a single system node.

Shared memory In parallel computers, an architecture in which there is a single pool of memory to which all processors have access.

SIMD Single Instruction stream, Multiple Data stream. This acronym describes distributed memory systems in which a single instruction stream is executed by all processors. This applies generally to array computers.

Speed-up A measure of parallel performance defined by the time required for one node to solve a problem executing the best sequential algorithm versus the time required for n nodes to solve it executing the best parallel algorithm.

Bibliography

S.L. Lillevik, "The Touchstone 30 Gigaflop DELTA Prototype," submitted to DMCC6.

M. Barton, E. Castro-Leon, E. Kushner, "ProSolver-SES™, a Skyline Equation Solver for the iPSC®/860," submitted to DMCC6.

E. Castro-Leon, M. Barton, E. Kushner, "Software Engineering Aspects of the ProSolver-SESTM Skyline Solver," Proceedings of DMCC5.

G. Withers (Intel Supercomputer Systems), R. Brown (U. of Washington), "High-Resolution Atmospheric Modeling on a Distributed Memory Supercomputer," submitted to Supercomputing 91.

M. Baber, "Hypertasking: Automatic Array and Loop Partitioning in the iPSC," Proceedings of the Twenty-Fourth Annual Hawaii International Conference on System Sciences, 1991.

W.L. Bain, "Air Traffic Simulation: An Object Oriented, Discrete Event Simulation on the Intel iPSC/2 Parallel System," Proceedings of the Fifth Conference on Distributed Memory Concurrent Computers, April 1990.

W.L. Bain, "Parallel Discrete Event Simulation Using Synchronized Event Handlers," Proceedings of the Fifth Conference on Distributed Memory Concurrent Computers, April 1990.

D.S. Scott (Intel Supercomputer Systems), C.C. Mosher (ARCO Oil and Gas Company), "A Parallel Implementation of 3D F-K Migration for Distributed Memory Computers," Nov. 1989 meeting of SEG.

S.L. Lillevik, "Systems Design and Engineering for Large-Scale Parallel Computers," Proceedings of Northcon 1989 Conference Record, Published by Electronic Conventions Management.

M.L. Barton, G.R. Withers, "Computing Performance as a Function of the Speed, Quantity, and Cost of the Processors," Proceedings of Supercomputing, 1989.

P. Pierce, "A Concurrent File System for a Highly Parallel Mass Storage Subsystem," Proceedings of DDMC5.

R. Asbury, D. Scott, "FORTRAN I/O on the iPSC/2: Is There Read After Write?," Proceedings of DDMC5.

G. Cheshire (Intel Supercomputer Systems), A. Jameson (Princeton University), "FLO87 on the iPSC/2: A Parallel Multigrid Solver for the Euler Equations."

M. Barton, "Three-Dimensional Magnetic Field Computations on the iPSC/2 Distributed Memory Multiprocessor."

M.L. Barton, E.J. Kushner, "Porting the ABAQUS Structural Analysis Code to Run on the iPSC/2," Proceedings of DDMC5.

W.L. Bain, "Aggregate Distributed Objects for Distributed-Memory Parallel Systems," Proceedings of the Fifth Conference on Distributed Memory Concurrent Computers, April 1990.

J. Brandenburg, M. Mirashrafi, J. McNamara, D. Billstrom (Intel Supercomputer Systems); E. Gilbert, M. Ferguson (Lucid, Inc.); A. Sizer, P. Alleyne (Artificial Intelligence Ltd.), "Advances in LISP for the iPSC/2."

D.S. Scott, E. Castro-Leon, E.J. Kushner, "Solving Very Large Dense Systems of Linear Equations on the iPSC/860," Proceedings of DDMC5.

S.L. Lillevik, "Touchstone Program Overview," Proceedings of DMCC5.

S.L. Lillevik, "DELTA: A 30 Gigaflop Parallel Supercomputer for Touchstone," Proceedings of Northcon 1990 Conference Record, published by Electonic Conventions Management.

D. Ecklund, "External Sorting on a Distributed-Memory Machine," Proceedings of DMCC6.

E. Castro-Leon, D. Scott, E. Kushner, "Block Gaussian Elimination on the Intel iPSC/860," Submitted to Siam University of Scientific and Statistical Computing.

E. Castro-Leon, D. Scott, E. Kushner, "Out of Core Dense Solver for Electromagnetic Problems," Presented at the International Conference on Industrial and Applied Mathematics. Contact Intel Supercomputer Systems Division for copy.

J. Hrenikoff, "Solutions of Problems in Elasticity by the Framework Method," *J. of Appl. Mechanics*, Vol. 8, 1941, pp. 169-175.

D. McHenry, "A Lattice Analogy for the Solution of Plane Stress Problems," *J. of the Inst. of Civil Eng.*, Vol. 21, 1943, pp. 59-85.

M. J. Turner, R. W. Clough, H. C. Martin and L. J. Topp, "Stiffness and Deflection Analysis of Complex Structures," *J. of Aero Sci.*, Vol. 23, 1956, pp. 805-823.

Index

ABOUT THE AUTHOR

Susann Ragsdale is a technical writing consultant with nearly 20 years experience in the electronics industry, ranging from integrated circuit process development through computer hardware and software development. Through her writing, she has been involved in CAE, electronic test equipment, and, more recently, the development of parallel computers of various types.